At Issue

What Is the Impact of E-Waste?

Other Books in the At Issue Series:

At Issue

What Is the Impact of E-Waste?

Cynthia A. Bily, Book Editor

GREENHAVEN PRESS
A part of Gale, Cengage Learning

GALE
CENGAGE Learning™

Detroit • New York • San Francisco • New Haven, Conn • Waterville, Maine • London

Christine Nasso, *Publisher*
Elizabeth Des Chenes, *Managing Editor*

© 2009 Greenhaven Press, a part of Gale, Cengage Learning.

Gale and Greenhaven Press are registered trademarks used herein under license.

For more information, contact:
Greenhaven Press
27500 Drake Rd.
Farmington Hills, MI 48331-3535
Or you can visit our Internet site at gale.cengage.com

For product information and technology assistance, contact us at

Gale Customer Support, 1-800-877-4253
For permission to use material from this text or product, submit all requests online at
www.cengage.com/permissions

Further permissions questions can be emailed to permissionrequest@cengage.com

Articles in Greenhaven Press anthologies are often edited for length to meet page requirements. In addition, original titles of these works are changed to clearly present the main thesis and to explicitly indicate the author's opinion. Every effort is made to ensure that Greenhaven Press accurately reflects the original intent of the authors. Every effort has been made to trace the owners of copyrighted material.

Cover image copyright Debra Hughes 2007. Used under license from Shutterstock.com.

LIBRARY OF CONGRESS CATALOGING-IN-PUBLICATION DATA

What is the impact of e-waste? / Cynthia A. Bily, book editor.
    p. cm. -- (At issue)
Includes bibliographical references and index.
ISBN-13: 978-0-7377-4118-6 (hardcover)
ISBN-13: 978-0-7377-4119-3 (pbk.)
1. Waste electronic apparatus and appliances--Management. 2. Electronic apparatus and appliances--Environmental aspects. 3. Refuse and refuse disposal. I. Bily, Cynthia A.
    TD799.85.W43 2008
    363.738--dc22
                                                            2008014669

Printed in the United States of America
1 2 3 4 5 6 7 13 12 11 10 09

Contents

Introduction

As of February 17, 2009, broadcasters in the United States no longer transmit analog television signals. For many consumers, the change to all-digital transmissions is insignificant: people who watch television through cable or fiber-optic systems, or through signals beamed to their homes and workplaces from satellites in space, are unaffected. Most newer televisions—including the popular high-definition TVs—are able to pick up digital signals. But the U.S. Government Accounting Office reports that thirty-eight million households in the United States own at least one television that still receives analog signals from an antenna, and twenty-one million households depend exclusively on analog transmission. That represents nearly one household in five. Families with televisions that receive analog signals have few choices if they wish to keep watching TV. They might buy, with financial help from the government, converter boxes that will allow their older televisions to receive digital signals. But what worries some environmentalists is the more likely choice: They will buy new televisions and throw away their old sets.

"There is going to be a huge spike in the number of TVs going into the waste stream," according to Barbara Kyle, national coordinator for the Electronics TakeBack Coalition. "It used to be that people would just demote their old TVs to somewhere else in the house, but I don't think that's the case here." Millions of televisions in the waste stream represent millions of pounds of hazardous materials that must be dealt with. Each set, for example, contains four to eight pounds of lead, according to the U.S. Environmental Protection Agency. That lead poses a serious health risk if it enters soil or water after being tossed in a landfill, or enters the air while being incinerated. Recycling by properly trained and equipped workers seems the most responsible disposal method, but many companies and municipalities choose the cheaper option of sending discarded electronics overseas to poor countries, where they are recycled under unsafe conditions.

Linda McFarland, executive director of a Michigan recycling company, has proposed that the Federal Communications Commission, the government agency that regulates broadcast communication, share the extra costs associated with getting rid of the analog televisions. A modest subsidy of four to five dollars per set—or a total of about $126 million— "would give the solid waste industry incentive to do the right thing and sort the TVs out of the regular garbage pickups instead of 'landfilling' them," McFarland says. Some cities now charge residents fees, typically ranging from ten to thirty dollars, to dispose of televisions and computer monitors, and some fear that rather than pay the fees, many people will dump their old analog sets in vacant fields or beside country roads.

The costs associated with safely disposing of millions of televisions are daunting. Some environmentalists believe that manufacturers must do more to produce electronics with less hazardous material, and to assume responsibility for their products when they break or become obsolete. Sony Electronics USA is the first television company in the United States to set up a recycling program. For no charge to consumers, Sony will accept any used product with the company name on it, and pledges to dispose of the electronics in a safe and responsible manner. Sony began with seventy-five drop-off sites across the country, and hoped to have 150 by the end of 2008. But other television manufacturers, anticipating the increase in discarded televisions, have lobbied Congress to pass the costs of recycling onto consumers.

The quarrel over what should happen to old televisions when the analog signals disappear is just the latest in a long series of local and national discussions about the disposal of out-of-date electronic equipment, or e-waste. As we become more and more dependent on televisions, computers, cell phones, digital cameras, and other devices—and as manufacturers create demand for new and better versions—we will continue to generate millions of tons of e-waste each year. As a responsible society, we will need to come to terms with several questions: What harmful materials are found in electronic devices, and might electronics be manufactured with safer alternatives? What are the most responsible ways to dispose of e-waste, and who should do that work? Who should pay the costs of responsible disposal? What can consumers do to reduce the harm that comes from the consumption of electronics? *At Issue: What Is the Impact of E-Waste?* addresses these and other issues that reflect the complexity and the importance of balancing our desire to enjoy the benefits of the electronic age with our responsibility to protect the Earth and each other.

1

Electronic Waste: An Overview

Elizabeth Royte

Elizabeth Royte is a journalist who writes frequently about the environment and whose work has appeared in national publications, including the New Yorker, *the* New York Times, National Geographic, *and* The Best American Science Writing 2004. *She is the author of two books, including* Garbage Land: On the Secret Trail of Trash *(2005), from which this viewpoint is adapted.*

Americans throw away millions of pieces of electronic equipment, including computers and cell phones, every year, and even those consumers who want to be careful about the environment are unsure of the best way to dispose of these devices. Sending electronics to landfills, incinerators, or recycling programs can release harmful chemicals that pose serious dangers to workers who handle such material. Even safe recycling is costly, and while countries in Europe have passed laws to require recycling, American citizens do not agreed about who should bear the cost in this country.

Electronic waste is accumulating faster than anyone knows what to do with it, almost three times faster than ordinary household trash. Researchers at Carnegie Mellon University estimate that at least 60 million PCs have already been buried in U.S. landfills, and according to the National Safety Council, nearly 250 million computers will become obsolete between 2004 and 2009, or 136,000 a *day*. Where will all these gizmos go, and what impact will they have when they get there?

Before I started studying garbage for my book *Garbage Land: On the Secret Trail of Trash*, I had no clue that the computer on my desk was such a riot of precious-but-pernicious materials. A cathode ray tube (CRT) monitor contains two to eight pounds of lead; e-waste, including CRT televisions, is one of the largest sources of this toxic heavy metal in municipal dumps. Printed circuit boards are dotted with antimony, silver, chromium, zinc, tin and copper. My computer, if crushed in a landfill, might leach metals into soil and water. Burned in a trash incinerator, it would emit noxious fumes, including dioxins and furans. Though scrubbers and screens would catch much of those emissions, scientists consider even minute quantities of them, once airborne, to be dangerous. Prolonged exposure to some of the metals in electronic devices has been shown to cause abnormal brain development in children, and nerve damage, endocrine disruption and organ damage in adults.

The processes that give birth to computers and other electronic devices are also cause for concern. A 2004 United Nations University study found that it takes about 1.8 tons of raw materials—including fossil fuels, water and metal ores—to manufacture a desktop PC and monitor. Mining, the source of the semiprecious metals in electronics, is the nation's largest industrial polluter; 14 of the 15 largest Superfund sites, designated by the Environmental Protection Agency as containing hazardous waste that poses a threat to people or the environment, are metal mines.

And we are a nation that has environmental laws. To supply the demand for new copper, gold, silver and palladium—stuff that fuels our 'lectronic lifestyles—African and Asian nations are tearing up their lands. Some gorilla populations in the Democratic Republic of Congo have been cut nearly in half as the forest has been cleared to mine coltan, a metallic ore comprising niobium and tantalum that is a vital component in cellphones. (A couple of leading cellphone companies have said they are trying to avoid using coltan from Congo.) Americans discard about 100 million cellphones a year, and though entrepreneurs refurbish and sell many overseas, and many cellphones in the United States are donated to charities, tens of millions of cellphones nonetheless end up in the trash.

The Complexities of Computer Recycling

Can a computer be recycled? I had a chance to find out when my network router quit connecting me to the Ethernet. I relegated this mysterious black box, the size of a hardcover book, to my basement until a local recycling group organized an e-waste drop-off.

Per Scholas' efforts keep some 200,000 tons of electronic waste from landfills and incinerators each year.

I arrived at the collection site, in Brooklyn, to find several folding tables shaded by white tents. They were laden with unwanted monitors, scanners, TVs, cellphones, keyboards, printers, mice and cables, many of which had absolutely nothing wrong with them beyond a bit of dust and, in the case of the computers, a processing speed that only yesterday seemed dazzling. Passersby pawed through the electronics casbah, free to take what they wanted. Per Scholas, a nonprofit computer recycler that supplies schools and other nonprofits with hand-me-downs, was allowed the leftovers. But its representative could only look on stoically as the good stuff—which he could refurbish and sell—disappeared. The bad stuff, like my router, was headed his way. So was I.

After climbing through a dim stairwell in Per Scholas' re-habbed brick factory building in the South Bronx, I walked through a low defile of shrink-wrapped computer monitors stacked upon wooden pallets. Angel Feliciano, the company's vice president for recycling services, led me into a large open room, where technicians wiped computer hard drives clean.

He told me that the reconditioned Pentium III—outfitted computers, collected from corporations and institutions that paid Per Scholas $10 a machine to haul them away, would be resold, at low cost, to "technology-deprived families." According to Feliciano, Per Scholas' efforts keep some 200,000 tons of electronic waste from landfills and incinerators each year.

Feliciano then took me to see the darker side of the computer recycling revolution, where monitors were being smashed, one by one, to smithereens. The broken-down (or merely out-of-date) Dells, Apples and Gateways trundled up a conveyor belt and into a shredding machine. Hidden inside the machine's carapace, magnets, eddy currents and tromel screens separated the shards and spat them into yard-high cardboard boxes: ferrous metals here, nonferrous there, plastic on one side, glass on the other. Feliciano said the metals went to a local company that resold them to smelters for separation and reuse; the plastic went to a company that pelletized it for resale. Disposing of the glass, which contains lead, presented the biggest headache.

Why is it so difficult to recycle computers properly? For starters, it is dangerous, labor-intensive and expensive.

"Glass is a liability, not a commodity," Feliciano told me. "We save it up until we've got a truckload, then we pay $650 a ton to a smelter who'll haul it away." Lately, the glass had been landing at the Doe Run Company, in south-central Missouri. The company recovers lead from glass through a process that begins with smelting and refining. One result is pure lead, made into 60-pound ingots, says Lou Magdits, Doe Run's raw-materials director. The company also salvages lead from car batteries, ammunition and wheel weights. And where does it all go? "Into car batteries, ammunition, wheel weights and new CRTs," says Magdits. (Doe Run operates a lead, copper and zinc plant in La Oroya, Peru. In 1999, that nation's Ministry of Health determined that 99 percent of the children in the area suffered from lead poisoning. The company, which bought the smelter from the Peruvian government in 1997, has entered into an agreement with the Health Ministry to reduce blood-lead levels in 2,000 of the most affected children and says that improved safety measures have decreased blood-lead levels in workers by 31 percent.)

Recycling Overseas

Per Scholas seemed to be handling my e-waste responsibly. But 60 to 80 percent of e-waste collected for recycling is shipped overseas, mostly to China, India and Pakistan, according to the Silicon Valley Toxics Coalition (SVTC), an advocacy group. Perhaps half of those computers are cleaned up and resold. But the remainder are smashed up by laborers, many of whom scratch for precious metals in pools of toxic muck. Investigators from SVTC and the Basel Action Network—formed after the 1992 Basel Convention, an international treaty that limits trade in toxic waste, which the United States declines to sign—videotaped men, women and children in the Chinese village of Guiyu extracting copper yokes from monitors with chisels and hammers. Squatting on the ground, they liberated chips and tossed them into plastic buckets. Black smoke rose from burning piles of wire. The workers, who wore no protective gear, reportedly swirled a mixture of hydrochloric and nitric acid—caustic, highly poisonous chemicals—in open vats, trying to extract gold from components. Afterward, they dumped the computer carcasses and the black sludge into fields and streams. Tests on the soil and water showed levels of lead, chromium and barium that were hundreds of times higher than those allowed by U.S. and European environmental health standards. The accumulating chemicals have contributed to high rates of birth defects, infant mortality, blood diseases and severe respiratory problems, according to Chinese media.

Why is it so difficult to recycle computers properly? For starters, it is dangerous, labor-intensive and expensive, and markets for the materials aren't always large or reliable. The incentives are for new production and the disposal or export of old components. Some computer manufacturers reportedly lobby to make "gray market" refurbishing illegal in developing nations where they sell new models. At the state level, governments spend bond money on incinerators and landfills, but most recycling centers have to balance the books on their own. Federal mining subsidies further skew computer economics. "If we were paying what we should for virgin resources, e-waste recycling would be much more economical, and local governments perhaps could break even on e-waste recycling," says Eve Martinez, a recycling activist in New York City.

As public awareness of the hazards of e-waste has risen, some computer manufacturers have begun take-back programs in which consumers wipe their hard drives clean and return the units to manufacturers. But the cost and the inconvenience to consumers discourage widespread participation. Computer retailers aren't wild about the idea, either. When I asked staffers at one of the largest computer merchants in New York City about taking back my gently used notebook computer, they said they didn't do it, didn't know anything about it and had never before been asked about it.

The European Union has adopted a directive requiring producers of electronics to recover and recycle e-waste.

Still, some states are forging ahead with e-waste reforms. Massachusetts bans televisions and computers from landfills. ElectroniCycle, a company based in Gardner, Massachusetts, processes the state's e-waste, recovering ten million pounds of components a year. Technicians refurbish 5 to 10 percent of the computers for resale; send another 5 to 10 percent to specialty repair houses; and smash the rest into 50 types of scrap, including plastic, copper, barium glass, and leaded and mixed glass. Reusable integrated circuits and memory cards are gleaned, while circuit boards are sent elsewhere for recovery of gold, palladium, silver and copper. In California, which bans e-waste from landfills and also from being shipped overseas, retailers that sell hazardous electronic equipment are now required to pay the state an "advanced recovery fee" (collected from consumers) of between $6 and $10 per device to cover recycling. Almost half the states have active or pending e-waste take-back legislation. Maine recently passed a law that will require manufacturers of computer monitors, video display devices and televisions to finance a system for environmentally responsible recycling.

European Programs Show Promise

In 2001, more than a dozen social justice and environmental groups formed the Computer TakeBack Campaign, which calls for manufacturers of anything with a circuit board to make "extended producer responsibility" (EPR) part of their credo. EPR would shift collection and recycling costs from taxpayers and government to companies, theoretically giving them an incentive to make computers and other gadgets that last longer, are made of reusable or recyclable materials, contain fewer toxics, and are shipped in less packaging. In Europe, EPR is gaining support. The European Union has adopted a directive requiring producers of electronics to recover and recycle e-waste. In Switzerland, the cost of recycling is built into the purchase price of new equipment; consumers return e-waste to retailers, who pass it on to licensed recyclers.

But in the United States, electronics recycling is in an awkward in-between stage, neither fully regulated nor completely understood by a tech-obsessed public that wants to do right by its e-waste. Still, there have been some recent improvements: spurred by U.S. advocacy groups and European nations that restrict the use of certain materials, computer manufacturers have reduced or eliminated some toxins in their products and made their computers easier to take apart. The Electronic Industries Alliance promotes recycling but opposes regulations that would make manufacturers alone bear the costs. The Consumer Electronics Retailers Coalition, which also promotes recycling, opposes systems, like that in California, in which retailers collect fees to cover recycling programs.

Speaking in 2002 at an industry trade show called Waste Expo, a Sony executive suggested dumping e-waste into open-pit hard-rock mines. One pit would hold 72 billion PCs—enough to make it worthwhile to mine the waste for copper, gold, iron, glass and plastics. Eyebrows were raised. Wouldn't deep pits of toxics-laced computers add insult to ecosystems that were already injured? Would miners extract the valuable metals using cyanide and arsenic, then walk away from what remained? The idea, mercifully, sank. Visionaries imagine a day when electronic devices are shipped back to their makers, who design all components with safe reuse in mind. Until then, maybe shoving the stuff in the basement or attic isn't such a bad idea after all.

2

Cell Phones Generate Particularly Dangerous E-Waste

Stan Cox

Stan Cox is a plant breeder and writer who lives in Salina, Kansas. He writes frequently about consumerism and health, and is the author of Sick Planet: Corporate Food and Medicine *(2008).*

As cell phones become smaller and more powerful—and as more people carry them—they create increasing dangers for the people who mine the rare metals that make the phones work and for the people who recycle discarded phones. Africa has seen violent conflict over the exploitation of miners and over the revenues generated by the sale of these metals. In the United States and Europe, consumers and manufacturers have discarded used phones irresponsibly, frequently dumping them in landfills or recycling them in ways that expose workers to toxic materials.

"As you crawl through the tiny hole, using your arms and fingers to scratch, there's not enough space to dig properly and you get badly grazed all over. And then, when you do finally come back out with the cassiterite, the soldiers are waiting to grab it at gunpoint. Which means you have nothing to buy food with. So we're always hungry."

That's how Muhanga Kawaya, a miner in the remote northeastern province of North Kivu in the Democratic Republic of

Stan Cox, "War, Murder, Rape. . . All for Your Cell Phone," *AlterNet*, September 14, 2006. www.alternet.org. Reproduced by permission.

the Congo (DRC), described his job to reporter Jonathan Miller of Britain's Channel 4 last year. Cassiterite, or tin oxide, is the most important source of the metallic element tin, and the DRC is home to fully one-third of the world's reserves. Some cassiterite miners work on sites operated directly by the country's military or other armed groups. Working in the same area are "artisanal" miners who are theoretically independent, like prospectors in America's Old West. But the cassiterite they extract is heavily taxed by the soldiers—when it's not just stolen outright.

With a land area as vast as that of Texas, California, Montana, New Mexico, Arizona, Nevada and Colorado combined, the DRC has only 300 miles of paved roads. To reach one of the many cassiterite mines in the virtually roadless northeast, 1,000 miles from the national capital Kinshasa, Miller's team followed a 40-mile footpath that, he reported, was as "busy as a motorway. Four thousand porters ply this route carrying sacks of rock heavier than they are. Each of their 50 kilogram packs of cassiterite is worth $400 on the world market. Government soldiers often force porters at gunpoint to carry the rocks free of charge; if they're lucky, though, they can make up to $5 a day."

So, why should we care? Because without cassiterite rock and the other ores mined in the Congo we would be unable to manufacture the linchpins of our global "weightless economy"—computers and telephones.

Greener Phones, Meaner Mines

A horrific war among the DRC military and various rebel armies officially ended in 2003 after taking 3 million to 4 million lives. But fighting continued long after that in the northeast, fueled by mining profits. First-ever democratic national elections in July [2006] have set up an October runoff election in the DRC, along with great hope for the future. Meanwhile, disarmament and integration of the armies is being carried out. But soldiers frequently receive little or no pay, and that provides a strong incentive for them to squeeze what they can from the cassiterite business.

The majority of the ore moves through illicit channels across the northeastern border to Rwanda, enriching troops and middlemen along the way. The U.K.–based organization Global Witness has comprehensively documented the impact of resource extraction in the DRC in a 2005 report that described "killing, rape, torture, arbitrary arrests, intimidation, mutilation, and the destruction or pillage of private property" that soldiers used "to gain control either over resource-rich areas or over the ability to tax resources."

In a cruel irony, Western efforts to make information-age products more environmentally friendly actually boosted incentives for violence and exploitation.

Since the July [2006] elections, says Carina Tertsaklan of Global Witness, "labor conditions remain pretty much the same, especially in the informal sector." She says the DRC government now has slightly more control over the mines, "but that's not necessarily for the better." Despite pressure from the United Nations and European Union to pay members of its newly integrated armed forces more consistently, miners are being treated just as they were during the war.

In a cruel irony, Western efforts to make information-age products more environmentally friendly actually boosted incentives for violence and exploitation. In late 2002, the EU [European Union] joined Japan in banning lead from the solder used in cell phones and other electronic goods. Traditional solder is an amalgam of 63 percent tin and 37 percent lead, but lead-free solder is composed almost 95 percent of tin. Partly in response to that new demand, the world price of tin shot up by almost 150 percent between August 2002 and May 2004, and has remained high since. As prices rose, fighting in the eastern DRC intensified.

Killer Coltan

This wasn't the first time that fighters in DRC and Rwanda have reaped a mineral bonanza. Back in 2000, a spike in the price of coltan, an ore that is the source of the precious metal tantalum, spurred feverish mining, profiteering and suffering in the same area of northeast DRC where cassiterite is mined. The DRC controls an estimated 64 to 80 percent of world coltan reserves, and the windfall from mining those deposits funded a Rwanda-backed rebel army of as many as 40,000 soldiers during 2000–2002. The mining was also blamed for destroying the habitat of the mountain gorilla; the gorilla population plunged by half in a national park where coltan was being mined.

Global demand for coltan increased with the growing use of tantalum in cell phones and other electronic devices. Whereas cassiterite is needed to make the products more eco-friendly, coltan is needed to make them more compact. Capacitors made with tantalum have an unmatched ability to hold high voltages at very high temperatures. Because of that, tantalum capacitors have been essential to the miniaturization of cell phones and other handheld wireless devices. At the time of the price spike, the No. 1 destination for the DRC's coltan exports was the United States. The prices of tantalum and its coltan ore have fallen from their 2000–2002 peak, but continued heavy demand from the electronics industry will keep their value high.

Getting a Signal—Halfway to the Moon

There's not much tin, and only a tiny amount of tantalum, in an individual cell phone; however, explosive growth in the wireless market has piled those metals up, milligram by milligram, into countless tons. In 2005, worldwide sales of mobile phones surpassed 200 million per quarter—that means that factories are churning out 25 phones every second, around the clock. Customers typically discard and replace their phones every 18 months in the United States, and that cycle is said to be down to 12 months in Western Europe.

In the spring of 2001, some analysts were expressing doubts over a seemingly outlandish prediction that 1.7 billion people—one out of every four on the planet—would be wireless subscribers by 2006. As it turned out, the planet now has more than 2 billion subscribers, and the industry [hoped] to sell a new phone to as many as of them as possible by the end of 2007.

Two billion of those little phones laid end-to-end would reach almost halfway to the moon. And that doesn't count the vast numbers already buried in landfills or abandoned in desk drawers.

As portable electronics acquire even more innovative features and (somehow) grow even smaller, their manufacture is sure to require even more exotic materials. And, more likely than not, those materials will come from some exotic location. Even before the handheld revolution, the United States was importing more than 70 percent of its tin, nickel, platinum and chromium, and more than 90 percent of its tantalum, aluminum ore, niobium and manganese. The EU and Japan are even more dependent on imports of those minerals, as well as silver, zinc, tungsten, gold, vanadium and copper....

Scary Old Phones

The level of exploitation continues to be affected much more by prices on the London Metal Exchange than by international efforts to protect workers or curb illicit trafficking of resources. Tertsakian says, "Organizations and journalists have created greater awareness, but I have to say we haven't seen that awareness translated into action." Even when Western manufacturers attempt to avoid buying Congolese minerals mined under deadly and exploitative conditions, they find it's not easy.

Demand for the minerals could be slashed if customers didn't replace their cell phones as often.

A great amount of the tin, coltan, copper and cobalt move out of the DRC via such roundabout and shadowy routes that it becomes almost impossible for a company at the end of the line to determine their origin. And human-rights-conscious consumers are even deeper in the dark. You can't boycott the assortment of metals in an electronic device the same way you can boycott a "conflict diamond" with a clearer history.

Demand for the minerals could be slashed if customers didn't replace their cell phones as often, and if when they did buy a new one, they no longer treated the old one as disposable. A myriad of for-profit and charitable organizations are now collecting unwanted cell phones for resale, donation or recycling.

Yet the U.S. Geological Survey (USGS) says that currently fewer than 1 percent of retired phones in this country are restored or recycled. With word spreading, that market may increase, and begin to affect the new phone market. As the title of an article in the [September 2006] issue of *Inc.* magazine shows, manufacturers are already concerned: "Three Scary Words: 'Buy It Used.'"

A 2004 California law requires sellers of cell phones to accept return of the instruments by their customers for reuse or recycling. It was passed in the face of the industry's intense nationwide efforts to defeat such mandatory take-back bills. Nationally, all four top wireless companies—Cingular, Sprint, T-Mobile and Verizon—have voluntary take-back programs;

however, a "report card" issued in April by the Washington, D.C.–based environmental group Earthworks gave those programs an F.

Of the Stores Earthworks visited, only 30 percent displayed information on drop-off and recycling, and only 50 percent of company representatives provided accurate information on the program. And companies could not verify that they were handling the returned phones according to best environmental and social practices, or that they weren't simply dumping many of them overseas.

Kimberlee Dinn of Earthworks says her group has seen some modest improvements in response to the report card. "There's a little more visibility of programs in the stores, more prominent mention on some of their websites. But not a single company has been able to provide us with statistics showing increased recycling of their phones."

If most used phones are being bought by people who would not have bought one otherwise, is reuse really cutting very deeply into demand for minerals?

To handle returned phones, all of the big four companies contract with ReCellular, Inc. of Dexter, Mich., which, according to Earthworks, is the only company to have been *removed* from the Electronics Recycler's Pledge of True Stewardship for noncompliance with its standards.

Dinn says California's mandatory recycling law has been a huge boon to ReCellular, which has grabbed 75 percent of the national market. CNN puts its market share somewhat lower, at 53 percent, and praises ReCellular for selling 55 to 60 percent of its still-functioning phones abroad, largely in poor countries where people can't afford new ones. That keeps waste out of U.S. landfills but also raises a question: If most used phones are being bought by people who would not have bought one otherwise, is reuse really cutting very deeply into demand for minerals, including those mined under conditions of near-slavery?

Tiny Treasure Trove

Once electronic goods go kaput (as they all eventually do), the metals they contain represent a potential "treasure trove," in the words of USGS. By their calculations, the 500 million phones now lying unused in American homes and businesses contain more than 17 million pounds of copper, 6 million ounces of silver, 600,000 ounces of gold, and 250,000 ounces of palladium.

The tin in the 110 pounds of cassiterite a hauler in Congo carries on his shoulders for 40 miles would make enough tiny drops of tin solder to manufacture tens of thousands of cell phones. The incentive to recycle that tin is boosted, of course, by the presence of precious metals lying next to it in the phone. But each device contains only a few cents' worth of any one metal, even the precious ones. And unlike aluminum cans, which are composed of a single, nearly pure metal, electronic goods don't surrender their diminutive, complex array of metals to the recycler without a struggle.

Among the charges that Earthworks levels at ReCellular has been that it ships nonusable phones to countries where hand labor for disassembly is cheap, but environmental and workers' rights abuses are commonplace. Dinn says, "You hear horrible stories from Malaysia, Sudan and other countries—no protective gear for workers handling the toxic materials in the phones, work being done by prisoners."

But Seth Heine, CEO of the phone recycling firm CollectiveGood in Tucker, Ga., says the metals in nonrepairable cell phones are well worth the costs of collection, shipping and processing, and that it can be done responsibly. Because CollectiveGood is "fixated on following absolutely the most environmentally sound procedures," Heine sends cell phones to an Antwerp, Belgium, company whose standards are "higher than anything in the U.S."

A seemingly insatiable hunger for mineral resources can and does distort economies in some of the planet's most desperate locales.

There, 17 different metals, including tin, copper, and cobalt, can be reclaimed. But says Heine, "No company's process at this point can reclaim tantalum. That's frustrating, considering its tragic history in the Congo."

On Their Backs

Reducing demand for coltan, cassiterite, heterogenite and other ores—by reusing, recycling, and simply not buying so damn many electronic goods so often—cannot by itself ensure safe jobs and living wages for people in the Congo or anywhere else. But a seemingly insatiable hunger for mineral resources can and does distort economies in some of the planet's most desperate locales. Relieving some of that distortion through reduced consumption at least gives nations and people a chance to build better lives independent of the ups and downs of world commodity exchanges.

Back in North Kivu last year, Channel 4's Jonathan Miller asked some of the people trudging along that muddy trail if they knew what the burdens they carried would be used for. He reported, "Not one of them knew their cassiterite was destined for the electronics industry in the rich world. One man claimed he knew: 'It goes to America,' he said, 'to rebuild the Twin Towers and the Pentagon.'" I don't know whether Miller told that man the real story—that within only a year or two, much of the tin in the rocks on his shoulders, having served its purpose in the information economy, would end up lying unused in a dresser drawer or trash heap.

3

Recycling of E-Waste Harms People Overseas

Anuj Chopra

Anuj Chopra, who lives outside Mumbai, India, is a journalist whose work has appeared in American publications, including the Christian Science Monitor *and the* San Francisco Chronicle. *In 2005 he won the CNN Young Journalist Award for print journalism.*

One solution for American companies wanting to dispose of e-waste inexpensively has been to ship old electronics to poor countries, where the labor costs for recycling or incinerating are much less. By one estimate, at least 75 percent of American e-waste is sent to Asia, where unskilled and unprotected workers disassemble machines by hand, exposing themselves to dangerous chemicals. Because every major new improvement in technology leads consumers to replace their electronics with newer models, the flow of e-waste appears to be increasing. Governments must outlaw the export of hazardous electronics to developing nations, and manufacturers must find ways to produce these products with fewer dangerous chemicals.

Once considered a problem that affects only industrialized nations, e-waste—pollution from the disposal of unwanted electronic and electrical equipment—is fast becoming a bane of developing countries.

Anuj Chopra, "Developing Countries Are Awash in E-Waste," *San Francisco Chronicle*, March 30, 2007, p. A-1. Copyright © 2007 *San Francisco Chronicle*. Reproduced by permission of the author.

Most e-waste in India is dumped in landfills or incinerated, releasing toxins into the air and soil that can cause cancer, birth deformities and arrested brain development, health experts say.

"We're sitting on an e-waste time bomb," said Shetty Sreenath, who built Asia's first eco-friendly e-waste disposal facility in 1995 in Bangalore, a southern city known as India's Silicon Valley.

Basel Action Network, a global watchdog on toxic trade based in Seattle, estimates that 75 to 80 percent of older machines from the United States wind up in Asian countries such as India and China, where recycling costs are much lower. The number of electronic products discarded globally has skyrocketed in recent years—50 million tons annually—and now makes up 5 percent of municipal solid waste worldwide, according to Greenpeace.

[In March 2007], the University of California signed an agreement not to send electronic equipment overseas or to state prisons to be dismantled or recycled. It also agreed to purchase only "green computers," those that are manufactured without hazardous materials. After an eight-month student campaign, the UC system is the nation's first university to accept such guidelines when purchasing electronic equipment.

If we go to sleep on this now, we'll end up badly polluting our environment and producing thousands of crippled children.

As the Indian economy has accelerated in recent years, consumers have been upgrading cell phones, computers, televisions, audio equipment, printers and refrigerators, annually churning out 146,180 tons of e-waste laden with chemicals, according to the International Resources Group based in Washington, D.C. These machines contain more than a thousand toxins, including beryllium in computer motherboards, cadmium in semiconductors, chromium in floppy disks, lead in batteries and computer monitors, and mercury in alkaline batteries and fluorescent lamps, according to Greenpeace. India is expected to triple its e-waste production within the next five years.

"If we go to sleep on this now, we'll end up badly polluting our environment and producing thousands of crippled children," said Sreenath.

Thuppil Venkatesh, director of the National Center for Lead Poisoning in Bangalore, says Indian hospitals are treating patients who have 10 times the normal level of lead in their blood. Lead affects the nervous system and brain development. Some of those patients are workers who eke out a living recycling e-waste by hand, without protective gear.

Selling secondhand parts to private computer assemblers is a thriving business in India—estimated at $1.5 billion annually—according to Toxic Link, a nongovernmental organization in New Delhi.

"We have seen (recyclers) breathing in dioxins as cables and casings burn around them," said P. Parthasarathy, a recycling expert in Bangalore.

In New Delhi alone, some 25,000 workers—including children—boil, burn or crush between 10,000 tons and 20,000 tons of e-waste annually. Electronic scrap yards also exist in the cities of Meerut, Ferozabad, Chennai, Bangalore and Mumbai, according to Toxic Link.

Governments and Industry Must Act

Both India and China are signatories of the Basel Ban Amendment of 1995, which outlaws the export of hazardous waste from industrialized nations to developing nations. Environmental groups say there are no statistics on e-waste because new and used machines are typically classified as electronics when exported.

The United States has signed—but not ratified—the 1992 Basel Convention, which calls on all countries to reduce exports of hazardous wastes to a minimum and to deal with waste problems within their borders. The United States has not signed the 1995 Ban Amendment to the Convention that formally incorporated an agreement to ban the export of wastes intended for recovery and recycling, nor has it passed legislation requiring U.S. companies to recycle their products or phase out the most toxic materials.

"High-tech companies do more than just sweep e-waste under the rug. They are sending it across the world in violation of international laws enacted to protect poor nations from the excesses of the world's wealthiest," said Ted Smith, founder of the Silicon Valley Toxics Coalition. "Every new generation of technology. . .sends zillions more of our computers and TVs to global trash heaps."

Sustained campaigns by environmental groups have already persuaded industry titans such as Hewlett-Packard, Dell, LG Electronics, Samsung, Sony, Sony Ericsson and Nokia to eliminate most hazardous materials from their products.

Microsoft's new operating system launched in January [2007]—Windows Vista—will make many older machines obsolete and create a "tsunami of e-waste" exported to developing nations, according to Jim Puckett, coordinator for the Basel Action Network.

"Much of stuff that is exported and turns up in India and China comes from local and state governments that are looking for the cheapest way to recycle," said Sheila Davis, executive director of Silicon Valley Toxics Coalition. "And there is a lot of material generated by multinational companies other than computer companies."

San Francisco delivers most of its e-waste to Norcal Waste Systems Inc., which subcontracts its recycling to E-Recycling of California. That company has accepted the Basel Action Network's "electronic recycler's pledge of true stewardship" to safely dispose of toxins and refrain from exporting hazardous materials to developing nations. San Jose uses ECS Refining LLC in Santa Clara, which has also taken the pledge.

Sreenath is India's first entrepreneur to build an alternative to landfills and incinerators. At his Bangalore company, electronics items are dismantled manually and by machines. Valuable components such as gold, platinum and aluminum are resold to electronics dealers. Sreenath says his company sells recyclable parts "down to the last screw."

Electronics companies need to produce greener electronics.

But Greenpeace activist Ramapati Kumar says such plants are mere palliatives.

"Electronics companies need to produce greener electronics. They need to clean up their products by eliminating hazardous substances, and recycle their products responsibly once [the devices] become obsolete," he said. "Most IT [information technology] companies show little interest in e-waste management because they fear it'll slow their growth."

In India, few firms are cracking down on e-waste.

Wipro Ltd., an IT behemoth listed on the New York Stock Exchange, [was] the first Indian electronics company to announce it [would] eliminate heavy metals from its products by June [2007].

"We are committed to phasing out toxic chemicals," said Gaurav Chaddha, Wipro's head of marketing.

Greenpeace's Kumar hopes Wipro will start a trend among Indian technology firms.

"More electronics companies need to come forward and commit to greener electronics," he said.

4

Loopholes in Recycling Laws Allow Toxic Dumping in Africa

Meera Selva

Journalist Meera Selva is a fellow of the Reuters Institute for the Study of Journalism and a visiting scholar of Green College, Oxford, England. She was Africa correspondent for the British newspaper the Independent *from 2003 to 2006.*

When a cargo ship unloaded 400 tons of dangerous chemicals in Abidjan, Ivory Coast, in 2006, thousands of people became seriously ill, and environmental groups were forced again to consider laws that protect poor countries from the toxic refuse of industrialized nations. E-waste—obsolete computers and other electronics—is commonly sent to Africa, China, and India for processing, often with no safeguards for those who live near landfills.

As they live near the biggest landfill in Abidjan [Ivory Coast], the people of Akouedo are used to having rubbish dumped on their doorstep. Trucks unload broken glass, rotting food and used syringes. Children try to make the best of their dismal playground, looking for scraps of metal and old clothes to sell for a few cents.

But this time, the waste would benefit no one. By [September 20, 2006], at least six people, including two children, had died from the fumes. Another 15,000 [sought] treatment for nausea, vomiting and headaches, queuing for hours at

Meera Selva, "Toxic Shock: How Western Rubbish Is Destroying Africa," *The Independent* (UK), September 21, 2006. Reproduced by permission.

hastily set up clinics. Pharmacies [ran] out of medicines and the World Health Organisation [sent] emergency supplies to help the health system. The Ivorian government resigned over the matter and, [by the next day], eight people [had] been arrested.

The tragedy is said to have begun on 19 August, after a ship chartered by a Dutch company offloaded 400 tons of gasoline, water and caustic washings used to clean oil drums. The cargo was dumped at Akouedo and at least 10 other sites around the city, including in a channel leading to a lake, roadsides and open grounds.

The liquids began to send up fumes of hydrogen sulphide, petroleum distillates and sodium hydroxides across the city. As the tidy-up operation [began], environmental groups [wondered] how this occurred.

A Longstanding Problem

"We thought the days when companies shipped toxic waste to poor countries were over," said Helen Perivier, toxics co-ordinator for Greenpeace. "It peaked in the 1980s but since then the determination of African countries to stamp the trade out has helped yield results. That this has happened again is extraordinary."

All down the West Africa coast, ships registered in America and Europe unload containers filled with old computers, slops, and used medical equipment.

Probo Koala, the ship that offloaded the waste, is registered in Panama and chartered by the Dutch trading company Trafigura Beheer. Trafigura had tried to offload its slops in Amsterdam, but the Amsterdam Port Services recognised its contents as toxic and asked to renegotiate terms. Trafigura said shipping delays would mean penalties of at least 250,000 US dollars (£133,000) so handed it over to a disposal company in Abidjan alongside a "written request that the material should be safely disposed of, according to country laws, and with all the correct documentation."

This story is a common one. All down the West Africa coast, ships registered in America and Europe unload containers filled with old computers, slops, and used medical equipment. Scrap merchants, corrupt politicians and underpaid civil servants take charge of this rubbish and, for a few dollars, will dump them off coastlines and on landfill sites.

Throughout the 1980s, Africa was Europe's most popular dumping ground, with radioactive waste and toxic chemicals foisted on landowners. In 1987 an Italian ship dumped a load of waste on Koko Beach, Nigeria. Workers who came into contact with it suffered from chemical burns and partial paralysis, and began to vomit blood.

Thereafter, the UN [United Nations] drew up plans to regulate the trade in hazardous waste through the Basel Convention. By 1998, the European Union had agreed to implement the ban, which prohibited the export of hazardous wastes from developed countries to the developing world, but the USA, Canada, Australia and New Zealand refused to sign up; global waterways are still filled with ships looking to unload their toxic waste.

The E-Waste Invasion Overseas

And now, there is a new threat—the dumping of electronic waste, or e-waste: unwanted mobile phones, computers and printers, which contain cadmium, lead, mercury and other poisons. More than 20 million computers become obsolete in America alone each year.

The UK [United Kingdom] generates almost 2 million tons of electronic waste. Disposing of this in America and Europe costs money, so many companies sell it to middle merchants, who promise the computers can be reused in Africa, China and India. Each month about 500 container loads, containing about 400,000 unwanted computers, arrive in Nigeria to be processed. But 75 per cent of units shipped to Nigeria cannot be resold. So they sit on landfills, and children scrabble barefoot, looking for scraps of copper wire or nails. And every so often, the plastics are burnt, sending fumes up into the air.

"There is a tradition of burning rubbish all over Africa, but this new burning of electronic equipment is incredibly dangerous," said Sarah Westervelt of the Basel Action Network, a pressure group that monitors the trade in hazardous waste. In China, workers burn PVC-coated wires to get at the copper, and swirl acids in buckets to extract scraps of gold.

We need to encourage people to think about whether they really need a new electronic item, and to consider what happens to the goods they throw out.

The United Nations Environment Programme estimates that worldwide, 20 million to 50 million tons of electronics are discarded each year. Less than 10 per cent gets recycled and half or more ends up overseas. As Western technology becomes cheaper and the latest machine comes to be regarded as a disposable fashion statement, this dumping will only intensify.

"Electronic goods are the fastest growing area of retail," said Liz Parkes, head of waste regulation at the Environment Agency. "We need to encourage people to think about whether they really need a new electronic item, and to consider what happens to the goods they throw out."

Where Does Our Rubbish Go?

- Inspections of 18 European ports in 2005 found that 47 per cent of all waste destined for export was in fact illegal.

- In 1993, there were two million tons of waste crossing the globe. By 2001, it had risen to 8.5 million.

- UK households throw away 93 million pieces of electrical equipment a year—about four items per household. Many of these end up in West Africa, India or China.

- There are more than 20 million redundant mobile phones in the UK.

- From summer [2007], manufacturers and importers of electrical goods will have to take responsibility for collecting and reusing old or outdated equipment.

- It is illegal to ship hazardous waste out of Europe, but old electronic items can be sent to developing countries for "recycling."

5

Prison Recycling Programs Are Dangerous for Inmates

Elizabeth Grossman

Elizabeth Grossman is an environmental journalist who lives in Portland, Oregon. In addition to writing articles for national environmental and news publications, she is the author of High Tech Trash: Digital Devices, Hidden Toxins, and Human Health *(2006).*

Because e-waste contains dangerous heavy metals, recycling electronics can be expensive. One cost-cutting measure that the United States has employed is using inmates in federal prisons—who earn less than the minimum wage—to dismantle monitors and televisions. These prison programs, however, are run without proper safeguards to keep workers from inhaling or ingesting dangerous materials, and inspections have shown that programs run by UNICOR, the common name for Federal Prison Industries, have exposed workers to harm.

About ten miles northwest of Merced, amid the dairy farms and orchards of California's San Joaquin Valley, sits the Atwater Federal Penitentiary, its tower and low-slung buildings the same mustard yellow as the dry fields that stretch out beyond the chain-link fence and concertina wire toward the Sierra Nevadas. Inside this maximum-security prison, inmates smash computer monitors with hammers, releasing dust that contains lead, cadmium, barium and other toxic substances. These inmates are employed by the electronics recycling division of Federal Prison Industries (better known as UNICOR).

Elizabeth Grossman, "Toxic Recycling," *The Nation*, v. 281, no. 17, November 21, 2005, pp. 20, 22, 24. www.thenation.com. Reproduced by permission.

With sales that nearly tripled from 2002 [to 2005], electronics recycling is UNICOR's fastest-growing business. But according to reports from prisons where this work is being done and interviews with former inmates employed by UNICOR, it's taking place under conditions that pose serious hazards to prison staff and inmates—and, ultimately, to the rest of America and the world.

In late 2004 Leroy Smith, Atwater's former safety manager, filed a formal complaint with the Occupational Safety and Health Administration. According to Smith, workers at Atwater's UNICOR facility are routinely exposed to dust from heavy metals. They were eating lunch in an area contaminated by lead, barium, beryllium and cadmium, he says, and using safety equipment that doesn't meet OSHA standards. Neither staff nor inmates were properly informed about the hazards, says Smith, who has more than a decade of experience with the Bureau of Prisons. After his superiors sent OSHA a report that downplayed and denied the problems, Smith sought whistleblower protection. . . .

With $10 million of revenue in 2004, seven prison facilities and about 1,000 inmate employees who [that] year processed nearly 44 million pounds of electronic equipment, UNICOR is one of the country's largest electronics recyclers. There are about 400 electronics recyclers in the United States—a burgeoning industry that is vital to solving one of the information age's peskiest problems. Americans own more than 2 billion pieces of high-tech consumer electronics. With some 5 to 7 million tons of this stuff becoming obsolete each year, e-waste is now the fastest-growing part of the US municipal waste stream. It's the most challenging mass-produced trash we've ever had to deal with.

Hidden Toxins Emerge

The cathode ray tubes (CRTs) in computer and television monitors contain lead, a neurotoxin, as do printed circuit boards. A typical desktop computer may contain up to eight pounds of lead. Mercury, another neurotoxin, is used in flat-panel display screens. Monitors contain cadmium, a known carcinogen. Circuit boards and exteriors use plastics containing flame retardants documented as disrupting thyroid hormone function and acting as neurotoxins in animals.

When high-tech equipment is intact, these substances are mostly harmless. But when digital devices are physically damaged—almost inevitable during disposal—the toxins emerge. By 2001 an Environmental Protection Agency (EPA) report estimated that discarded electronics accounted for 70 percent of the heavy metals and 40 percent of the lead in US landfills. Synthetic chemicals used in electronics have been found in people, animals, food and household dust all around the world.

Given the hazards posed by landfilling and incinerating high-tech electronics, the safest way to dispose of them is to separate their materials, which can then be reprocessed as feedstock for new products. But these materials are tightly packed, largely unlabeled and of variable design, making that separation process both expensive and labor intensive.

The Prison Solution

That's where UNICOR comes in. The United States—unlike the European Union and several other countries, including Japan—has no national laws requiring electronics recycling. Yet over the past few years, individual states and local governments have begun enacting legislation to keep high-tech trash out of their landfills. At the same time, a growing number of businesses and organizations, concerned about the liabilities posed by dumping old computers, are opting to have equipment recycled. To save money many are sending equipment to UNICOR.

"UNICOR's program is labor intensive, so capital machinery and equipment expenses are minimized, this helps keep prices low," says a company brochure. With a captive work-force UNICOR's electronics recycling program can afford to be labor intensive. Because it is run by the Bureau of Prisons, UNICOR does not have to pay minimum wages—recent wages were $0.23 to $1.15 an hour—or provide benefits. Though UNICOR is not taxpayer supported, its pay scale would not be possible without taxpayer support of the inmates.

The savings pay off for UNICOR: In 2004 UNICOR's Lewisburg, Pennsylvania, prison facility won a contract from the Pennsylvania Department of Environmental Protection with a price one-quarter of that bid by private-sector recyclers. "I welcome the competition, but let's level the playing field," says Andy Niles of Scientific Recycling in Holmen, Wisconsin. Niles says he had to lay off about one-quarter of his staff after losing business to his state's prison industry.

Instead of investing in state-of-the-art disassembly equipment and durable safety gear, UNICOR reportedly distributed ball-peen hammers and cloth gloves.

"Busting up monitors exposes you to a lot more risk. But broken monitors saves on shipping costs," says Greg Sampson of Earth Protection Services, another private recycler. "Broken, you can fit about 100 into a carton, whereas only thirty-five or so will fit if they're intact. We don't break ours up." Neither do other private recyclers I contacted. "It's more expensive, but we pack them in lined boxes that are shipped with a manifest indicating hazardous material contents, and we use special machines to deactivate CRTs," explains Scott Sodenkamp, operations manager at the Noranda Recycling plant in Roseville, California. At Atwater, Leroy Smith told me, broken CRTs are packed in cardboard cartons and sealed with plastic wrap.

Unprotected Workers

UNICOR doesn't just save money by busting up monitors and paying prison wages. Instead of investing in state-of-the-art disassembly equipment and durable safety gear, UNICOR reportedly distributed ball-peen hammers and cloth gloves to inmates working at Atwater. "The gloves ripped easily and there were lots of bad scratches and cuts," a former Atwater UNICOR worker told me. Staff and inmates who worked at UNICOR's Elkton, Ohio, and Texarkana, Texas, operations have similar accounts of broken glass, noxious dust and injuries resulting from inadequate tools.

UNICOR declined my request to visit the Atwater facility. But an OSHA inspector who toured it in late 2004 confirmed many of the inmates' complaints: "While conducting sampling, I observed, and numerous workers reported, the improper use of tools and techniques due to the lack of appropriate tools to more safely dismantle monitors."

UNICOR's computer disassembly process releases so much lead, in fact, that its dust qualifies as hazardous waste.

"We were given light-particle dust masks and the stuff would get in behind them," the former Atwater inmate told me. "In the glass-breaking room, guys would be pulling junk out of their hair and eyebrows. We were coughing up and blowing out all sorts of nasty stuff, and open wounds weren't healing." The coveralls inmates wore on the job—kept on during breaks and meals—would come back from laundering with glass and metal dust in rolled cuffs, he says. Work boots were worn outside the factory, too, potentially contaminating other areas of the prison—something OSHA regulations are designed to avoid. Prison staff, say Smith and others, wear regular uniforms and shoes in the factory, allowing contaminated dust to be transferred to their cars, homes and families.

Contaminated Air and Work Surfaces

In 2002, air samples taken at Atwater found lead levels twice OSHA's permissible exposure level, and cadmium ten times the OSHA standard. Wipe samples found lead, cadmium and beryllium (which causes severe lung disease) on work surfaces and inmates' skin. Blood and urine testing found barium, cadmium and lead, some at elevated levels.

UNICOR's computer disassembly process releases so much lead, in fact, that its dust qualifies as hazardous waste. Smith and former staff at UNICOR's Elkton, Ohio, facility say this waste has been improperly handled. "Prison staff were removing the filters that collect the dust from the glass-breaking without wearing respirators, and putting these filters in the general prison trash," says Smith, who showed me photographs of worktables covered with thick layers of pale gray dust.

Because UNICOR works behind bars, it has another advantage over its competitors: It doesn't have to be prepared for unannounced OSHA inspections. And even though some factories opened in 1997, there were no OSHA inspections until 2004. The air tests in late 2004 found lead, barium and cadmium at Atwater—but below the levels at which OSHA requires the use of safety equipment. These test samples, however, were not taken around inmates "involved in the deliberate breaking of computer monitors," says the OSHA report. Even so, barium, beryllium, cadmium and lead were found on work surfaces; barium, cadmium and lead were found in the workers' dining area, creating the potential for accidental ingestion. But none of that violates OSHA standards. As the OSHA inspector noted, there are actually "no standards or regulatory levels for these metals on surfaces."

How toxic is the dust? Long-term exposure to low levels of cadmium damages kidneys and can lead to lung disease. Workers exposed to the levels of lead found in Atwater's air in 2002 would eventually have elevated blood lead levels—not enough to cause acute lead poisoning but plenty to cause kidney or neurological damage, according to leading environmental and occupational health scientists. "If a workplace has enough lead to fall near the OSHA standards, that would be enough to come home and pose a risk to children," says Howard Hu, a professor at the Harvard School of Public Health.

Inhalation exposure is the most dangerous in terms of getting lead into the body, Hu says. OSHA standards—and those now set by the EPA—likely allow far higher exposure than is truly safe. In fact, says Dr. Bruce Lanphear, director of the Children's Environmental Health Center at Cincinnati Children's Hospital Medical Center, "there is no safe level."

Government Must Demand Accountability

Despite the recent surge of concern about data security, most people know little about where discarded digital equipment ends up. Great quantities of e-waste sent to domestic recyclers end up overseas—in China, Africa, Southeast and South Asia, and other developing regions—where much of it is processed cheaply, under unsafe and environmentally unsound conditions. To avoid this, many recyclers and their clients demand rigorous documentation of the downstream flow of dismantled equipment.

"Environmental stewardship and social responsibility are critical issues for our clients," says Robert Houghton of Redemtech, which recycles electronics for Fortune 500 companies. Redemtech considered working with UNICOR, Houghton told me, but chose not to because UNICOR could not provide the downstream accountability Redemtech's customers required.

UNICOR says that no material it recycles will be landfilled or exported for dumping. UNICOR's no-export policy prohibits shipping electronic waste to any country barred by the US government from receiving US products. These countries, UNICOR told me, are Cuba, Iran, Iraq, North Korea, Libya, Sudan and Syria. But that leaves many countries to choose from, since US laws only prohibit exporting hazardous material destined for disposal—rather than recycling—or when it involves transfer of "sensitive" technology. "It's absolutely legal to send this stuff to Pakistan," says Houghton.

The United States is the only industrialized nation that uses prison labor for electronics recycling.

Much of what UNICOR recycles comes from the federal government, which buys about 7 percent of the world's computers and disposes of at least half a million each year. In 2002 the Defense Department sent some 17 million pounds of used electronics to UNICOR for recycling. UNICOR's website also lists several universities as clients. But some counted as customers no longer are—among them the University of Colorado, which wanted better documentation than UNICOR provided. Same with Johns Hopkins. "Using prison labor was not looked at very favorably," says a university employee who asked not to be named.

The United States is the only industrialized nation that uses prison labor for electronics recycling. "We can do without it, but are we willing to do without it?" asks Craig Lorch, whose company, Total Reclaim, is among the thirty or more that have pledged not to use prison labor. Until environmental and social benefits are given priority over the bottom line, UNICOR's low-cost option will continue to be used by the government and many others. But relying on workers who are not paid a living wage, and who work in unhealthy and environmentally unsound conditions, displaces rather than solves the e-waste problem. The long-term environmental costs cannot even be calculated. As long as the United States does not require transparency and accountability from recyclers, it will be impossible to know how these toxic materials are treated, or where they go.

6

E-Waste Could Contribute to Global Warming

Mark Hall

Mark Hall is editor at large for Computerworld, *a weekly magazine for information technology executives. He writes a column about new and upcoming products and is a frequent commentator on technology issues for the mainstream media.*

Global warming is now widely recognized as a serious problem caused by the use of fossil fuels. Although the use of computers has, in many ways, reduced the consumption of petrochemicals, information technology executives also need to be aware of the environmental impact of the electronics they discard. When buying new equipment, executives should ask about energy efficiency and eventual disposal.

Unless you've been summering in Antarctica, in which case you experienced the phenomenon firsthand, you've seen the news coverage indicating that global warming is now considered a serious issue. Scientific studies, such as the prestigious and conservative Intergovernmental Panel on Climate Change 4th Assessment Report released [in February 2007], point to human activity as an undeniable contributor.

Even Doubter-in-Chief President [George W.] Bush mentioned global warming concerns in his [2007] State of the Union address. It seems you have to be a member in good standing of the Flat Earth Society to doubt the human effect on the Earth's climate.

Mark Hall, "E-Waste Not," *Computerworld*, v. 41, no. 8, February 19, 2007, p. 20.

Information Technology and Petrochemical Consumption

The scientific consensus is that the release of greenhouse gases through the consumption of fossil fuels causes global warming. Like every industry, IT [information technology] plays a part in this process. And as a growing industry, IT will be consuming more and more, and therefore contributing more and more to global warming and other types of environmental degradation. Just consider PCs. Gartner [an IT research company] estimates that in the next three years, 400 million will be replaced worldwide. That's a lot of plastic, glass, metals and chemicals to dispose of, with all of their attendant environmental effects.

It can be argued that IT helps other industries reduce their resource consumption by making, say, petrochemical processes more efficient. And IT makes it possible for people to work remotely, cutting down on resource consumption by individuals. Although I can't prove it, I believe that without IT, the effects of climate change would be worse today, and much worse in the near future.

When IT buys gear from vendors, neither party gives much thought to the environmental aftereffects.

But let's not delude ourselves. Computers and networks come with environmental costs. IT devices can be resource-intensive to produce and difficult to dispose of properly.

It's time to add environmental factors to the total cost of ownership [TCO] calculation for every IT hardware purchase. Right now, when IT buys gear from vendors, neither party gives much thought to the environmental aftereffects. Can you imagine being compelled to upgrade to a new car every five years and then having to either give the old one away or pay someone to take it because its net value was effectively zero and it required special handling to recycle? That's the situation CIOs [chief information officers] are in with hardware.

Executives Should Demand Accountability

But imagine if IT executives started to include environmental issues in TCO. They not only would ask how energy efficient a vendor's devices are but would also demand specifics on the disposal of the gear at the end of its useful life. They might even probe as to whether the widgets under scrutiny were produced in an environmentally sound manner. The answer might not be a deal breaker (and let's face it, many an IT vendor's sales force would be clueless about how the gear they peddle is put together), but just asking such questions would send a message to high-tech manufacturers: All other things being equal, I will choose the more environmentally conscious company.

By and large, CIOs do a pretty good job of minimizing the environmental effects of their IT assets. Today's tight budgets actually help here, since you buy technology only when you need it. But beyond that, many of you pay for the proper disposal of old computers. Some of you donate hardware to non-profits and schools. Others offer obsolete gear to employees. A large number of you hire asset-disposal firms to recycle your stuff. To me, that sounds like the "reduce, reuse, recycle" credo in action.

One more action—making hardware's environmental effects part of your TCO calculation—seems like a logical and necessary step. It's time to take it.

7

European Regulations Prove That E-Waste Can Be Managed Responsibly

Henrik Selin and Stacy D. VanDeveer

Henrik Selin, who studies hazardous substance management, is an assistant professor in the Department of International Relations at Boston University. Stacy VanDeveer conducts research on international environmental policy making, and is an associate professor of political science at the University of New Hampshire.

As international trade has made electronic products available to consumers around the world, the e-waste generated by these devices also has become an international problem. The European Union (EU), through its passage of three important sets of regulations, has become the world leader in handling hazardous substances responsibly. Because the EU represents so many potential customers, many international manufacturers have begun to make changes in the ways they produce electronics so that their products will meet EU standards. The United States government, on the other hand, has remained strongly opposed to this kind of policy making, arguing that it stifles competition and innovation.

As a result of expanding international production and trade, a consumer in Berlin, Boston, Beijing, or Bangalore can choose between many similar manufactured goods in

Henrik Selin and Stacy D. VanDeveer, "Raising Global Standards," *Environment*, vol. 48, no. 10, December 2006, pp. 6–18. Copyright © 2006 by Helen Dwight Reid Educational Foundation. Reproduced with permission of the Helen Dwight Reid Educational Foundation, published by Heldref Publications, 1319 18th Street NW, Washington, DC 20036-1802.

her local store. For example, she can purchase a cell phone, laptop, freezer, stove, or vacuum cleaner made by a large multinational company that is a household name around the world. Similarly, environmental activists in San Francisco, Shanghai, Surat, and Stockholm might share a growing concern about the ecological and human health risks posed by discarded electronic and electrical products—so-called e-waste, which contains myriad hazardous susbstances that present significant environmental and human health problems.

The European Union (EU) has emerged as a global leader on hazardous substances policy. While such policy has been a cornerstone of EU environmental policy since the 1960s, the EU has recently developed a series of new policy initiatives to further address negative environmental and human health impacts of hazardous substances. These new policies govern the use, recycling, and disposal of hazardous substances in electronic and electrical products and expand regulations on the production, use, and sales of tens of thousands of chemicals. While these policies regulate the management of hazardous substances and e-waste across 27 European countries, EU policy also increasingly shapes decisions by policymakers, manufacturers, and consumers around the world.

The EU is increasingly replacing the United States as the de facto setter of global product standards.

Three recent EU policy developments—two "directives" and one "regulation," in EU terms—are of particular significance to the future management of hazardous chemicals and e-waste. The first directive covers waste electrical and electronic equipment (WEEE), and the second outlines restrictions on the use of certain hazardous substances in electrical and electronic equipment (RoHS). WEEE and RoHS entered into force in February 2003. Finally the regulation on the registration, evaluation, and authorization of chemicals (REACH) [became] legally binding in 2007.

WEEE, RoHS, and REACH are noteworthy for several reasons. All are critical for EU sustainable development efforts. Furthermore, aspects of the new hazardous substances and e-waste standards are the highest in the world. As such, they are drawing considerable attention from policymakers, regulators, company managers, and environmental activists from around the globe. Because of growing international trade and the diffusion of policy ideas and information, producers and users of chemicals, heavy metals, and manufactured goods in markets such as the United States, Japan, and China will be affected by EU policy. In effect, new, higher EU regulatory and product standards are likely to push many global standards upward through a process that political scientist David Vogel calls "trading up.". . .

International Markets and Economic Influence

With a population of nearly 500 million and an annual market of about $11 trillion there are few large multinational companies that do not operate or sell their products in the EU. Regulatory standards set in Brussels can have significant implications for international production and trade. If non-EU firms want to continue to sell their products in the EU, they will have to comply with EU product rules and standards. Most firms operating in multiple markets prefer to produce their products to as few different standards as possible, and they often follow the highest regulatory standard. This is particularly likely for products where major producers compete across markets. For example, if HP or Dell needs to redesign their laptops or substitute chemicals used in their production to meet EU standards, WEEE, RoHS, and REACH may also affect laptops made and bought outside the EU.

This international market-based influence of WEEE, RoHS, and REACH reflects a broader change in global standard setting. Historically, many product standards for consumer and environmental protection were set in the United States because of the size of the U.S. economy and the stringency of early U.S. standards. Whereas U.S. chemical policy in the 1970s and the early 1980s often acted as an inspiration for European policymaking, the EU has taken over the role as leader in chemical policy development. The EU is increasingly replacing the United States as the de facto setter of global product standards, and the center of much global regulatory standard setting is shifting from Washington, DC, to Brussels. New EU policies—and similar policies being enacted in response in other parts of the world—are also engendering responses in international markets.

In other words, the importance of WEEE, RoHS, and REACH extends far beyond the EU border through processes of international economic integration and trade. One U.S. engineer recently noted that RoHS "is probably the biggest change in electronics in 50 years" for the United States (and global) electronics business. A recent report also suggests that the costs to U.S. firms for complying with REACH are far lower than the benefits of continued and expanding transatlantic trade. This suggests they must adjust and absorb the costs of doing so. In addition, a rapidly growing market in consulting services to help producers comply with the growing array of national and international regulations has emerged. Such services are likely to quickly diffuse information about the new EU chemical and waste policies and the responsibilities they place on firms operating in or exporting to the European market.

International Political Influences

Policy ideas and information about environmental and human health risks travel across borders. They do so in part because individuals and organizations with similar values and interests import and export information and ideas for strategic purposes. For example, policymakers, regulators, and environmental or consumer advocates might ask why, if certain substances are deemed too risky for use in Europe, are they still being used in the United States or China? Similarly, if firms can afford to collect their used electronic products in Europe for recycling and/or disposal, some actors will ask why they oppose such responsibilities in the United States or elsewhere. In fact, such questions are already being asked, and the politics of chemical and e-waste management already show signs of change well beyond EU borders.

Many non-EU governments look to the EU for policy guidance about hazardous substances and e-waste management. For example, in 1908, Japan enacted legislation on the recycling of household appliances that requires industry to establish a recovery and recycling system for discarded products. Yet the EU is now tackling the issue of e-waste more broadly. Because much of Japanese environmental legislation tends to follow EU legislation, Japan may look to the EU for further policy guidance on how to improve hazardous substances and e-waste management. China—the world's largest producer of cellular phones and color TVs—is in the process of developing and implementing RoHS-like legislation, which, after some delays, [was] scheduled to enter into force in 2007. China has also expressed interest in copying ideas underpinning REACH. In addition, South Korea is in the process of finalizing its own national RoHS legislation modeled after the EU's.

Together, the U.S. government and industry organizations have lobbied intensively against these EU policy developments.

European actors also want other jurisdictions to adopt similar chemical and waste policies. Now that EU standards have increased, European officials, European environmental organizations, and European firms have shared interests in exporting EU standards to other countries and in uploading such standards into international agreements. Political scientist David Vogel argues that such shared interests lead to coalitions of environmental actors and firms—"Baptists and bootleggers"—that use market forces to "trade up" regulatory standards. This is consistent with a long-standing EU strategy, dating from the first Environment Action Programme in 1973, of active engagement in international forums to achieve goals that could not be obtained solely at a regional level. As such, the EU can be expected to pursue the uploading of its new chemical and waste management policies in a host of international forums.

U.S. Policies Are Less Stringent

In the United States, recycling legislation is largely left to the discretion of states. Some states with a high concentration of high-tech industries such as California, Florida, New York, Oregon, Texas, Virginia, and Washington have taken legislative measures on e-waste that go beyond federal U.S. regulations with an eye toward the latest European policy developments. In 2003, California passed an electronic waste recycling act that bans the sale (after 1 January 2007) of electronic devices that are prohibited under RoHS. In 2006, New York City Council members debated whether to require producers of a long list of electronic products to set up a city-wide take-back system. Several U.S.–based companies, including Apple, AT&T, HP, IBM, and Motorola, are also involved in WEEE management in the United States and internationally. In addition, California and other states looking to strengthen their chemical policies are closely following developments in REACH.

The EU and the United States are the two main global producers and users of chemicals: Europe accounts for more than one-third and the United States accounts for one-fourth of global chemical production with extensive transatlantic trade in chemicals. Furthermore, the EU and the United States are also large generators of e-waste. Together, the U.S. government and industry organizations have lobbied intensively against these EU policy developments, targeting the European Commission, the European Parliament, and national politicians and policymakers. Yet while U.S.-based firms have lobbied European officials extensively over REACH and other proposals, they typically do not carry the same political influence in Brussels and other European capitals as they do in Washington, DC.

Despite this interest in EU policy developments from U.S. states, municipalities, and firms, the U.S. federal government and some industry organizations have been fierce critics of WEEE, RoHS, and, in particular, REACH. Reflecting some of their major criticisms, the U.S. State Department and the United States Mission to the European Union distributed a report by the National Foreign Trade Council in 2003 on several EU policy developments, including WEEE, RoHS, and REACH, that argued:

> The EU has invoked the precautionary principle, a non-scientific touchstone, to justify its identification and assessment of such risks as well as its enactment of technical measures to manage and eliminate them. By doing so, it has effectively banned U.S. and other non-EU exports of products deemed hazardous, stifled scientific and industrial innovation and advancement and, in the process, has ignored a basic reality, namely that a certain amount of risk is unavoidable in every day life.

Needless to say, the European Commission and many European politicians and policymakers strongly reject these claims. EU officials assert that the precautionary principle is not "non-scientific" but an indispensable principle for guiding decisionmaking on risk under conditions of uncertainty regarding effective environmental and human health protection. WEEE, RoHS, and REACH are also designed to stimulate technical innovation to reduce the use of hazardous substances and make recycling and disposal of e-waste easier. In addition, the European Commission argues that all recent EU legislation is compatible with the rules of the World Trade Organization.

From a European perspective, "better living through chemistry"...will require higher regulatory standards to more effectively manage chemical hazards and e-waste.

Although the [President George W.] Bush administration and the U.S. chemical industry continue in their strong opposition to much EU environmental policymaking, a growing number of other countries, U.S. states, and private firms are looking to the EU for inspiration and practical suggestions for better management of hazardous substances and e-waste. Once WEEE, RoHS, and REACH are fully operational, they are likely to further influence international production and regulatory standards. REACH, for example, will generate massive amounts of information about chemicals and is likely to improve the ability to comparatively assess the risks or various chemicals. Environmental advocates in the United States, China, and many other places will pay close attention to such information.

Further Challenges Ahead

Like the burning of fossil fuels, the use of chemicals and heavy metals has radically improved human life, making it considerably less "nasty, brutish, and short," even as they pose severe ecological and human health risks. The same can be said for the growing use of electronic products, which results in mountains of e-waste. A critical question before public, private, and civil society actors concerns how best to preserve and enhance the tremendous gains in human well-being made for many of us from the use of chemicals, heavy metals, and modern technology, while engendering more environmentally and socially sustainable outcomes. From a European perspective, "better living through chemistry"—to cite the old Du-Pont slogan—will require higher regulatory standards to more effectively manage chemical hazards and e-waste.

Ongoing EU efforts to deepen economic and political integration, raise regulatory standards, and promote sustainable development are guided by a series of EU-wide strategies, action programs, and policies adopted in recent years. Critics have argued, however, that some of these efforts may not be compatible. For example, EU economic policies tend to promote Western-style consumption while EU environmental policy supports waste minimization and recycling. In this respect, the EU—and all member states—faces the critical challenge of formulating and implementing a coherent strategy for promoting economic growth that is socially and environmentally sustainable. Nevertheless, as the EU seeks to do this, policymakers, regulators, corporate managers, environmental and consumer activists, and consumers not just in Europe but across the globe will be affected.

8

Businesses Can Handle E-Waste Without Government Interference

Dana Joel Gattuso

Dana Joel Gattuso, of Alexandria, Virginia, is an environmental policy analyst with the Competitive Enterprise Institute, a non-profit public policy organization that supports free enterprise and limited government. She has written several articles and opinion columns about electronics recycling.

An increase in the use of electronics has caused many people to worry unnecessarily about the disposal of such equipment. Environmentalists have claimed that e-waste is a growing and toxic problem, and have encouraged the government to step in with regulations and fees to handle what activists see as a dangerous situation. But manufacturers have a good record of handling computer waste on their own, and as long as they are responsible for recycling and disposal, they will have a strong incentive to find better and cheaper ways to do it. The government should step aside and let industry handle e-waste.

The widespread use of computers in the home and the rapid technological advancements that enable new, better, and more powerful models to roll out each year have created an enormous number of obsolete machines. The annual number of used, outdated personal computers increased from 18 million in 1997 to an estimated 61 million in 2004. Experts

Dana Joel Gattuso, "Mandated Recycling of Electronics: A Lose-Lose-Lose Proposal," Competitive Enterprise Institute, February 1, 2005. www.cei.org. Copyright © 2005 Competitive Enterprise Institute. Reproduced by permission.

[predicted] that from 2004 to the end of 2007, there [would] be a total of 246 million home computers no longer in use.

To date, most used computers have not yet entered the waste stream. An estimated 75 percent are likely stored in people's homes in attics, garages, and basements. Fourteen percent are believed to be recycled or reused, and an even smaller amount—11 percent—is landfilled. The issue of what to do with the increasing amount of electronic waste (e-waste) is a growing concern, particularly as consumers start disposing of their machines.

The swirl of hype and misinformation. . .is creating enormous confusion and fear in the world of waste management policy.

Exacerbating the challenge is the rapid spread of misinformation that is creating an unwarranted near-panic among policy makers who fear there is no adequate policy in place for handling the growing amount of waste. Most of these fears are based on the following false claims:

- E-waste is growing faster than the municipal waste stream, and will overtake the available landfill space.

- Toxics contained in computers and other electronics are leaking out of the landfills and poisoning our ground soil and groundwater.

- Our goal should be zero-waste to save our natural resources and protect the environment.

The swirl of hype and misinformation, coming largely from environmental activist organizations with a goal of generating nothing short of "zero waste," is creating enormous confusion and fear in the world of waste management policy, distracting policy makers from identifying the real problem and seeking a proper solution. Worse, misperceptions are generating misguided policies that only intensify the problem. For example, a number of states' recent rush to ban television sets and computers from municipal landfills is creating an even larger problem in deciding how to handle the growing amount of waste.

State and federal lawmakers, believing that the answer lies in recycling mandates, increasingly are embracing "extended producer responsibility" policies—which require manufacturers and retailers to take back and recycle or refurbish their used equipment—and "advanced recovery fee" approaches—which tax consumers to fund government-run e-waste collection and recycling operations. Some lawmakers are also considering "eco-design" mandates stipulating what materials manufacturers can and cannot use to ensure easier recyclability.

Mandated recycling and "green design" requirements would be disastrous. The costs are staggering and will ultimately be passed down to consumers. New design and recycle requirements will cripple technological innovation, and widespread recycling and substance bans will unleash a host of unintended environmental and health risks.

Almost all manufacturers have in place some sort of a system to collect and recycle their used products.

The problem of how to handle the nation's electronic waste stream is a challenge, not a crisis. The growth in the amount of waste is expected to stabilize in just a few years. Most of it can be handled in today's modern landfills, which are built to contain hazardous as well as non-hazardous waste safely. The remaining amount of e-waste can be managed through the continued recycling—and, more importantly, the reuse and donation—efforts of manufacturers, retailers, recyclers, and nonprofits. But for this to occur more extensively and successfully, government must get out of the way and end its regulatory barriers. . . .

Manufacturers Operate Their Own Programs

Long before EPA [U.S. Environmental Protection Agency] launched its e-waste recycling campaign and before some states began mandating recycling, a number of electronics manufacturers were already running their own recycling programs. These early efforts were geared toward collecting and recovering systems from business customers. More recently, manufacturers have begun to set up programs to address e-waste in the home. Today, almost all manufacturers have in place some sort of a system to collect and recycle their used products.

At a time when state and local governments are struggling to fund electronic waste recycling efforts—and financing these efforts on the backs of taxpayers and/or consumers—manufacturers are voluntarily running their own collection and recycling programs, providing a service to their customers, and competing with other players in the market.

Round Rock, Texas–based Dell, the world's second largest computer manufacturer, has been operating its own computer take-back and recycling program since 1991. The program, called Asset Recovery Services, provides Dell's business customers with the option of reselling used computer systems and recovering the value of the equipment or recycling the systems if they no longer have value. Dell also provides businesses with the option of leasing computer equipment, which ensures the computer systems will be returned to the manufacturer at the end of their use.

In 2002, Dell expanded its recycling services to include used computers from residences. For $15 a unit, Dell will pick up a used computer of any brand. The company will arrange to have it either recycled or donated through the National Cristina Foundation, a nonprofit charity organization that provides used computers to disadvantaged children and adults. Dell will also give customers rebates for trading in a used computer for a new one.

Through these promotions, as well as a national recycling tour that enabled 9,000 residents in 17 cities to bring their used computers to a designated location, Dell collected a record 35 million pounds of computer waste during its fiscal year 2004. Dell set a goal to increase the amount collected in weight by 50 percent [in 2006].

Palo Alto, California–based Hewlett-Packard (HP), the world's biggest computer manufacturer, recycles and refurbishes its used machines in-house, running one of the largest recycling plants in the world. According to HP, the company has recycled more than 500 million pounds of electronic waste since its recycling program started in 1987. Each year, HP reports, it collects about 80 million pounds of used products. During its fiscal year 2004, HP recycled 42 million pounds—an annual increase of 3 million pounds—and pledged to reach 1 billion pounds of recovered or recycled waste by 2007. Like Dell, HP will take back computers from any manufacturer, not just HP. The company charges anywhere from $13 to $34 per unit, depending on the type of equipment.

The nation's leading computer and electronics manufacturers. . .now know how best and most effectively to take them apart.

Gateway, based in San Diego, pays its customers for their old computers. Purchasers of new systems receive a $50 rebate for trading in the old one. According to Gateway's executives, "It's a win-win. It drives sales for us, and it takes PCs out of the basements and storerooms."

Manufacturers Have Flexibility and Creativity

The nation's leading computer and electronics manufacturers, by running their own recycling programs for some time now, have developed skills beyond designing and constructing new computers: They now know how best and most effectively to take them apart. No two take-back and recycling programs are the same. Companies are testing and devising methods that best work for them, their contractors, and their customers.

Furthermore, because companies are in the driver's seat, they are continuously looking for ways to improve their recycling and reuse programs, making it easier for customers to return used products, and finding ways to collect and break down the used equipment more cost-effectively. As Dell Sustainable Business Director Pat Nathan told *The Dallas Morning News*, Dell is looking to "analyze data from suppliers and customers to develop more efficient recycling methods, eventually recycling computers at a lower cost than its competitors can and offering customers a lower price." Over time, these companies are learning how to cut costs. As a result, the collection fees that manufacturers charge consumers have remained constant or even declined—with some companies like Dell, Gateway, and HP providing customers with rebates for trading in used computers.

By contrast, local governments attempting to operate electronic collection and recycle services for residents are struggling, prompting states to enact fee programs to come to their rescue. But even the fees, which have risen on average by 40 to 100 percent since 2001, are failing to cover the costs.

Some argue that these recycling and reuse efforts by the private sector do not even come close to addressing the millions of obsolete electronics that are entering the waste stream each year. Yet this argument fails to acknowledge the enormous achievements the industry has made in a relatively short time. [In 2004], Dell, HP, and IBM collectively recycled 160 million pounds of computers and computer equipment. This figure doesn't include the number of units remanufactured for donations and reuse.

If the growing trend is for government to impose its own set of rules on how manufacturers should build and take apart electronics, producers and recyclers will be forced to abandon what works for them and follow a new set of rules. A burgeoning private marketplace of creative ideas and innovations, where producers compete to provide the best collection service at the lowest possible cost to the customer, will be replaced by a government bureaucracy that has no particular incentive—or ability—to keep costs down.

What's the Problem?

Before we consider a possible solution, we first have to identify the problem. Despite panic over the e-waste "crisis," the real problem with obsolete computers and electronics seems to depend on who you ask. As Resources for the Future resident scholar Margaret Walls writes, "In discussions about policies directed at electronic waste, one often finds that participants have different views on policy objectives—i.e., different views on exactly which environmental problems. . .should be the focus of policy."

For example, some policy makers' concerns center around the rapid increase in the amount of discarded electronics— fears that waste is growing at an uncontrollable rate and that we are running out of landfill space. A related concern is how local and state governments are going to handle the increasing number of discards. Others worry about the lead used in CRTs [cathode ray tubes, used in televisions and monitors] and fear that it and other heavy metals are not safely contained in landfills. Most media reports play off public fears of lead and other toxics seeping into the ground soil and drinking water.

EPA officials, however, assert that our municipal landfills safely contain the lead, mercury, and other metals. Their concern is over the issue of sustainability, troubled that we are not addressing the environmental impacts of these products and the natural resources they consume throughout their life cycle. Similarly, environmental pressure groups argue that the growing amount of electronic waste reflects the ills of a "throw-away" society, and that the recycling of all electronics is our moral obligation in helping to achieve "zero waste tolerance."

This is consistent with the observation. . .that the directives never specifically articulate an environmental problem but state that the objective is to save natural resources. As Jacques Fonteyne of the European Recovery and Recycling Organization in Brussels notes, "The debate has been inappropriately centered on the idea that the aim of EU [European Union] waste policy should be 'to maximize recycling.' We argue that the aim should be 'to minimize the environmental impact.'" These are two very different policy goals that require very different policy actions.

Policy makers have a responsibility to look hard at the evidence on computer and electronic waste and determine if there is a real problem.

The confusion and inability to reach a consensus on identifying the problem is not surprising given the amount of baseless facts and misinformation flying around about e-waste. Lawmakers are responding to a lot of conflicting information without knowing if used electronics truly pose a problem and, if so, what the actual problem is.

Policy makers have a responsibility to look hard at the evidence on computer and electronic waste and determine if there is a real problem. If a problem is identified, it is crucial to know if the solution can be achieved without unleashing problems of its own. The types of policy decisions now being debated—and in some cases, enacted—have been shortsighted. These new laws carry extremely high costs, and their consequences carry their own health and environmental risks, as has been discussed throughout this report.

Landfill Capacity and Safety

It is true that the number of obsolete electronics is growing and will continue to grow as new and improved systems replace the old, and systems now gathering dust in attics and basements enter the waste stream. But the growing quantity of waste is not an insurmountable problem. The same data on increasing quantities of e-waste cited by environmental activists also show that the annual number of obsolete computers will peak *this year* [2005]—at 63.4 million units.

Contrary to popular belief, landfill capacity in the United States is plentiful. A single 120-foot-deep, 44-square-mile landfill could accommodate the United States' garbage for the next 1,000 years—that's less than one-tenth of 1 percent of the land in the U.S. Furthermore, landfill capacity is not diminishing but remains fairly constant, according to the EPA. While many landfills have been closing due to stringent federal regulations, these represent only 8 percent of all capacity. New landfills are on average 25 times larger than the older landfills they are replacing.

Landfill limitations are primarily due to political constraints, not physical ones. As archaeologist and anthropologist William Rathje, the author of *Rubbish! The Archaeology of Garbage*, wrote in *Smithsonian* magazine, "The United States has plenty of space for solid waste disposal for centuries to come; the political decision of which particular spaces to use is the problem." Finally, a ton of waste costs only $40 to landfill, another indication of the abundance of landfill space, compared to a staggering $500 to recycle.

Without question, computer and TV monitors containing lead, cadmium, mercury, and other hazardous materials should be handled with care. But, given the modern design, required piping systems to carry out leachate, and extensive monitoring system of today's landfills, there is no reason to believe that landfills are ill-equipped to handle hazardous materials in e-waste. In fact, some experts believe recycling computers and TVs carries far greater health and environmental risks due to emissions from lead smelters in the recycling process, "compared to the small likelihood that a [computer monitor] would ever leach lead in a. . .lined landfill."

9

Recycling of Electronics Can Be Done Safely

Mark Clayton

Mark Clayton is a staff writer for the Christian Science Monitor.

Obsolete consumer electronics, or "e-waste," represents less than one percent of total municipal solid waste, but its environmental impacts are far reaching. Recycling efforts for e-waste, or "e-scrap," are still in their infancy, but there are still ways for consumers to recycle electronics safely. Organizations such as the Environmental Protection Agency and The National Recycling Coalition provide information and services, as do manufacturing companies. You can also donate obsolete or out-of-fashion computers and cell phones to organizations that will give them to someone in need, such as victims of domestic violence.

Among America's 140 million cellphone users, Mia Shabazz is typical. She's got one phone gathering dust in a drawer, another in her purse that's about to join the one at home, and a third she's set to buy right now.

Peering into the glass case of a cellphone sales display, one of five scattered around a Boston shopping mall, Ms. Shabazz bobs on her toes with excitement.

"That one's kind of cute—I think I want a flip phone," she says.

Plucking it out of the display case, a T-Mobile salesman hands it to her along with his pitch: When she changes phones

Mark Clayton, "Electronics of Christmas Past are Coming Back to Haunt U.S. Landfillers," *Christian Science Monitor*, January 2, 2004. Reproduced by permission from *Christian Science Monitor* (www.csmonitor.com).

next time, she can just remove a chip inside this one and put it in her new phone—no need to reprogram all those numbers.

That's handy. But it also keeps environmentalists like Eric Most lying awake at night, wondering what will happen to those hundreds of millions of "old" cellphones. Indeed, all those tiny phones, along with VCRs, faxes, televisions, and the growing profusion of electronic devices, are producing a slow-motion avalanche of obsolete consumer electronics or "e-waste."

E-Waste a Growing Problem

The problem could spike early next year as holiday shoppers snap up new cellphones and digital TVs, computer monitors, and cameras—sending the conventional models on a slow trek to the closet, and then to the dump. Alternatives such as recycling or reuse are in their infancy, at least here in the United States. In all, about 3 billion units of consumer electronics will be scrapped through 2010, predicts a new report by the International Association of Electronics Recyclers.

"Americans already have a large inventory of obsolete consumer electronics sitting in their homes," says John Powers, a consultant to the electronics recycling industry, adding, "The pace of technological change in consumer electronics seems to be growing. So in five years, that buildup is going to be significant."

So far, e-waste represents less than 1 percent of total municipal solid waste, the Environmental Protection Agency reports. But the fraction belies its potential pollution impact.

More than other municipal solid waste, e-waste is larded with heavy metals that leach into groundwater. Chromium, zinc, lead, copper, manganese, selenium, and arsenic are common on electronic circuit boards. The threat from those is growing as the volume in landfills grows.

Consider cellphones. Though tiny, they add up to a big pollution threat because they have the shortest lifespan among consumer electronics—1.5 years—according to a report last month by INFORM, an environmental group.

Most of the phones still work, but are technologically or fashionably obsolete. That means that by 2005, an estimated 100 million more cellphones will join the 400 million on their first stop before the dump—in drawers or basements.

Last month's ruling by the Federal Communications Commission could accelerate the trend. The FCC is allowing cellphone subscribers to switch carriers—and take their phone numbers with them. Phones can be reprogrammed, but many are not compatible with the new company's equipment. So it's often less expensive for companies to issue a new phone.

Bottom line: The move is expected to generate up to 30 million more obsolete phones, containing lead and beryllium, that could head to the dump. The metals leach into groundwater, points out Mr. Most, author of the INFORM report.

Computers may represent an even bigger problem. Some 300 million to 600 million personal computers in the US could be headed to dumps in the next few years—many of them overseas, says Ted Smith, executive director of the Silicon Valley Toxics Coalition. The group estimates that up to 80 percent of old computers end up being exported to places like China or Vietnam, where children and peasants pick apart the toxic innards for $1 a day.

Demand for New Electronics Contributes to Toxic Waste

Although the US has signed the Basel Convention prohibiting export of toxic waste, Congress has not ratified it (joining Afghanistan and Haiti as the only countries not honoring the treaty), Smith says. So toxic container loads of computers, televisions, and cellphones are sent abroad.

It's not just the dropping cost that's accelerating the tech turnover, it's fashion, says Danielle Levitas, consumer research analyst for market research firm IDC. "We're starting to see people buying not out of necessity, but because something is newer, bigger, or flatter."

Indeed, flatter was the rage this Christmas and is likely to be for several years with flat-screen video display prices dropping fast.

The switch could accelerate because of another FCC ruling, which sets 2006 as the year for the US to leap to digital television. That alone will turn the 230 million to 280 million cathode-ray tube (CRT) televisions in US homes into dinosaurs and begin their march toward the dump, Ms. Levitas and others warn.

Less than 1 percent of the millions of phones discarded annually are recycled for raw materials or refurbished.

That's bad because CRTs contain four to eight pounds of lead shielding that can easily leach into groundwater, environmentalists and state officials say. Four states—Massachusetts, California, Maine, and Minnesota—now prohibit landfilling CRTs. More are likely to follow. The result: more exports of CRTs abroad, Smith says.

Recycling Electronics Safely

Recycling efforts for e-waste, or "e-scrap" as the 400-plus member electronics recycling industry calls it, are still in their infancy. Just one-tenth of e-waste, about 200,000 tons a year, gets recycled. And, while thousands of donated used cellphones have found their way into the hands of the needy or are resold, less than 1 percent of the millions of phones discarded annually are recycled for raw materials or refurbished, INFORM says.

Eventually, the private sector could boost recycling in a big way. But so far, state and federal efforts have fallen short, environmentalists charge.

To fix the problem in the long run will require increased durability, standardized design, designs that facilitate disassembly, and reduction of toxic components. The ultimate solution, Smith says, would be for the federal government to require manufacturers to take financial responsibility for the products from beginning to end.

The faster pace of electronic obsolescence means the [recycling] business expects to quadruple in size by 2010.

That approach, already mandated in Europe, would give them incentives to design products with less hazardous materials and make them more recyclable. But environmentalists agree the US remains significantly behind in dealing with its mounting e-waste problem.

Recycling electronic components, or "e-scrap," is a big business still in its infancy. In the past decade, the industry has grown to $700 million and more than 400 companies. The faster pace of electronic obsolescence means the business expects to quadruple in size by 2010, according to the International Association of Electronics Recyclers. While most programs are geared toward corporate recycling, there are several programs for consumers:

Recycling Programs for Consumers

- Electronics recycling: Go to the Environmental Protection Agency's e-waste site: www.plugintorecycling.org. The National Recycling Coalition has helpful information at: www.nrc-recycle.org/resources/electronics/links.htm.

- Cell phones: They can be a lifeline for victims of domestic violence. To donate your phone, go to the "Wireless Foundation" site: www.wirelessfoundation.org. Or go to www.recyclewirelessphones.org for another list of options.

- Computers: Manufacturers are starting to offer recycling programs. For Dell, go to www.dell.com click on "home and home office," then scroll to the "recycle" button. For Hewlett Packard, go to www.hp.com, click on "home and home office," then type "recycle" into the search box. Check with your manufacturer for other programs.

For details on how to donate a computer, go to www.tech soup.org, click on "products," then "recycled hardware," and go to the link: "Ten Tips of Donating a Computer." After that, you can click on "Donate Hardware" to find a list of recyclers near you.

Warning: Be sure you erase personal information saved on your hard drive before you donate or recycle to avoid identify theft.

10

The Federal Government Should Help Pay for Recycling E-Waste

Ron Wyden

Ron Wyden is a United States senator from Oregon. He is a member of the Senate's Committee on Energy and Natural Resources and chairs its Subcommittee on Public Lands and Forests. In the following viewpoint, Wyden describes the Electronic Waste Recycling and Promotion and Consumer Protection Act of 2005, a bill he cosponsored but that was never enacted.

Our nation's ever-growing amount of e-waste is hazardous if not handled properly. The best way for the federal government to encourage the proper disposal of electronics is to offer financial incentives for consumers and businesses that recycle. Incentives for recycling, rather than fees and other punishments for not recycling, will motivate people to change their behavior. But if a nationwide recycling plan is to be created, we must have nationwide regulations, rather than a series of different laws for different cities and states.

M r. Chairman, America is a computer-dependent society. I'm willing to bet that before coming to this hearing, almost every person in this room used a computer to write a document, to check e-mail, or to read the news. Yet as much as we depend on our computers, we seldom think about what they're made of. Let me tell you.

Ron Wyden, testimony before Senate Committee on Environment and Public Works Subcommittee on Superfund and Waste Management, July 26, 2005. http://wyden.senate.gov.

The desktop computer in your office right now contains about 14 pounds of plastic, 4 pounds of lead, 8.5 pounds of aluminum, more than 12 pounds of iron, half a pound of nickel and lesser amounts of arsenic, cadmium, mercury, titanium, zinc, beryllium and gold. There's mercury in LCD and gas plasma screens, lead in monitors and circuit boards, cadmium in chip resistors and semiconductors and heavy metals in CPUs. And every year, millions of newly obsolete computers—and televisions, and other electronic trash or e-waste—are discarded to the tune of 2.2 million tons. Those 2.2 million tons of e-trash are the equivalent of 219 Boeing 737 jetliners. If handled improperly, this hazardous stew of toxic e-waste can poison water supplies, people and the environment. But there is a better way.

Incentives for Recycling

Today, barely one in 10 computers gets recycled or reused. Compare that to old cars: 94 percent goes to scrap yards where useable parts are reclaimed, and the rest of the material is shredded, compacted and recycled into appliances, cars and other products.

Senator [Jim] Talent [of Missouri] and I believe that the United States can put less e-waste in the landfill and more in the recycling bin. We have proposed S. 510, a pro-consumer, pro-environment and pro-technology bill to jumpstart a nationwide recycling infrastructure for electronic waste. Our bipartisan approach is the first to rely on incentives, rather than upfront fees or end-of-life penalties, to deal with electronic waste. Our legislation offers incentives to consumers and small businesses to get their old computers and laptops out of the closet and into the e-waste stream. Our legislation offers manufacturers, retailers and recyclers incentives to to recycle e-waste. The bill has the support of retailers, electronics manufacturers, and environmental recyclers.

Specifically, our legislation would:

- Establish an $8 per unit tax credit for companies that recycle at least 5,000 display screens or computer system units per year;

- Establish a $15 tax credit for consumers who recycle their old computers and TVs, provided they use qualified recyclers;

- Prohibit the disposal in a municipal solid waste landfill of any electronic equipment with a display screen larger than 4 inches or any computer system unit, beginning three years after the bill passes if EPA [Environmental Protection Agency] finds that the majority of U.S. households have reasonable access to e-waste recycling;

- Modify EPA's universal waste rule to classify screens and system units as "universal wastes" to allow for easier collection, processing, transportation and recycling;

- Require federal executive agencies to recycle or reuse their display screens and CPUs; and

- Direct EPA to recommend to Congress the feasibility of establishing a nationwide e-waste recycling program that would preempt any state plan within one year.

One nationwide program seems to make the most sense.

We do not claim to have a monopoly on the wisdom for how e-waste should be recycled, and so the tax credit is limited to 3 years. Our goal is to get a recycling infrastructure launched, and in the meantime, have EPA look at various options, at what various states are doing and come up with recommendations for Congress for a natiowide e-waste recycling plan.

A National Program Is Necessary

The bill recognizes that states like California have already put a plan in place, and that many other states, like Oregon, are moving in that direction. But if every state and hundreds of municipalities and counties take different paths to solve the e-waste problem, the country will end up with a hodgepodge of rules and regulations. Companies and consumers who are keen on doing the right thing will be confused, innovation will be stifled and not a lot of recycling would get done. One nationwide program seems to make the most sense.

Last week the *New York Times* carried a story about computers so infected with spyware and adware that they are on life support. Rather than going through the painstaking process of debugging them, consumers opt to toss them out and pay several hundred dollars for a new one. Unless some miracle cure is found, the spyware plague is not going away anytime soon, and the number of discarded computers will grow.

Then there's the transition to digital television, which could pull the plug on analog television sets in 21 million American households. The handover of the old analog channels could take place in the next 4–5 years. Unless the U.S. gets serious about recycling electronic trash, what is going to happen to all those old TV sets?

It is not very often Congress has the chance to get a jump-start on solving a problem. This is one place where a bipartisan effort can make a real difference. I look forward to working with you to get a nationwide electronic waste recycling program launched.

11

Manufacturers Should Pay for Recycling Their Products

Joel Denbo

Joel Denbo is chief manager of operations for Tennessee Valley Recycling LLC of Decatur, Alabama, a family-owned-and-operated scrap processor. In 2005, when he delivered the congressional testimony that appears as the following viewpoint, Denbo chaired the Institute of Scrap Recycling Industries, a trade organization representing hundreds of companies.

Recycling is an important part of the U.S. economy because it provides raw materials for industry while saving energy. Some members of the Institute of Scrap Recycling Industries have a long history of recycling electronics, and they have learned to distinguish "scrap," or materials that can be reused, from "waste," or materials that must be thrown away. But scrap processors can make a profit only if the markets for reusable materials stay strong, and government-imposed regulations and taxes on recycling will drive up its cost. Instead, manufacturers should absorb some of the cost of recycling the products they manufacture.

Mr. Chairman and members of the subcommittee, my name is Joel Denbo. I am here as chair of the Institute of Scrap Recycling Industries (ISRI). ISRI is the trade association that represents 1,260 private, for-profit companies that process, broker and industrially consume scrap commodities including metals, paper, plastics, glass, textiles, rubber and electronics at nearly 3,000 facilities worldwide—over 80% of

Joel Denbo, testimony before House Committee on Energy and Commerce Subcommittee on Environment and Hazardous Materials, September 8, 2005.

those facilities are located in the United States. Approximately 300 of our 1,260 members handle electronics, either exclusively or as an aspect of their other recycling activities. I am also the third generation leader of Tennessee Valley Recycling, a company my family began in 1907 that currently has plants located in Alabama and Tennessee.

In the minds of many, recycling in the United States is a phenomenon that began in the 1970s following the original Earth Day celebration. For others, awareness dates to the late 1980s following the infamous voyage of the "garbage barge" and the ensuing fears that landfill capacity had reached a crisis stage. It may interest the committee to know that the scrap recycling industry actually dates back to the beginnings of our nation, when a statue of King George III was toppled in NYC [New York City], and its metal was used to make bullets for the Continental Army. Our members are in the business of recycling and have formed the basis of the established recycling infrastructure that exists in this country today.

The costs of recycling [electronics] are more than the value of the component materials that can be extracted from them.

Scrap Recyclers Contribute to Industry

Today, the processing of scrap commodities is an integral part of the U.S. economy and its domestic manufacturing industries. Scrap commodities are collected for beneficial reuse, conserving impressive amounts of energy and natural resources in the recycling process. For example, according to the Environmental Protection Agency, recycled aluminum saves the nation 95 percent of the energy that would have been needed to make new aluminum from virgin ores. Recycled iron and steel result in energy savings of 74 percent; recycled copper, 85 percent; recycled paper, 64 percent; and recycled plastic, more than 80 percent. Collectively, ISRI members process over 130 million tons of recyclables each year, worth upwards of $30 billion and contribute more than $2 billion annually to the U.S. balance of trade. . . .

ISRI members have been recycling electronics for decades as an integral part of their recycling operations. Indeed, early computers—mainframes as they were known—were highly sought-after commodities in our industry. In 2002, recognizing the ever-growing number of obsolete personal computers and peripherals, and other electronics materials entering the recycling stream, ISRI formed an Electronics Council to address the issues unique to this segment of the scrap recycling industry's activities. Sensing an opportunity, as good businessmen and entrepreneurs generally do, many of our member companies are investing significant capital to expand their businesses to recycle more electronics. Yet, while they have acted on their "recycling know-how" and sense of opportunity, they also know that before electronics recycling can stand on its own, a number of challenges familiar to the traditional scrap recycling industry need to be addressed.

The challenges include, among other things, the need to distinguish between scrap and waste, to develop end-use markets for the materials recovered from scrap electronics, to promote manufacturer design improvements to make electronics easier to recycle and to avoid the use of hazardous materials in the manufacture of electronics products, and to promote the benefits of environmental management systems, such as ISRI's Recycling Industry Operating Standard (RIOS) as the proper means to address environmental concerns. Consequently, ISRI's Board of Directors [in August 2005] adopted a policy resolution outlining how best to address these challenges.

As businessmen who know how to recycle, our views are derived from years of practical experience. In order to assist this committee's efforts to understand how best to ensure that electronics are recycled properly, and not disposed of in landfills or elsewhere, I would like to highlight some of the key issues within our policy.

Scrap Is Not Waste

We need to avoid creating unnecessary impediments to recycling. Thus, it is very important to distinguish the difference between scrap and waste. Electronics scrap, like scrap paper, glass, plastic, metal, textiles, and rubber, is not waste. Scrap is the opposite of waste. Processed scrap materials are commodities that have a value on domestic and international markets, whereas waste materials have no value and are typically buried in a landfill. Electronics recyclers make their living by providing de-manufacturing services, such as scrubbing and reselling hard drives, by reselling cell phones, monitors, and CPUs that are in good working order, and by using machinery and equipment to shred or otherwise process electronics to extract the various commodities that are in electronics, like steel, aluminum, gold, silver, titanium, copper, nickel, plastic, and glass.

Defining obsolete electronics as waste undermines and overlooks the value that these electronics retain if properly recycled. Saddling them with the moniker of waste imposes a whole host of unwarranted regulatory burdens that will undermine the ability to make the system work. For these reasons, it is eminently important that we avoid confusing these valuable commodities with wastes.

Another key aspect underlying our policy is the concept of free and fair trade. We have been in the recycling business a long time and understand that scrap commodities are some of the best examples of basic supply-and-demand economics. These materials are traded in the global marketplace, supplying America's basic manufacturing industries with valuable raw material feed stocks that are used in place of virgin materials, and contributing significantly to the United States' balance of trade with other nations. Hence, our industry has generally opposed efforts to interfere with commodity markets and create artificial distortions. However, being the pragmatic businessmen that we are, we recognized that the electronics market has grown explosively in such a short period of time that, for the short term, it might take some sort of financial mechanism to ensure that the costs of recycling electronics— which sometimes have a "negative intrinsic value"—do not deter recycling from taking place.

Electronics manufacturers have taken some steps toward designing for recycling; however, there is room for improvement.

Allow me to explain. Right now, under current market conditions, if a citizen, a governmental entity, a commercial or retail establishment wants to do the right thing and recycle their electronics, recyclers must charge that citizen or other entity a fee in order to justify the costs of recycling certain obsolete electronics components, such as older computer monitors and TVs with cathode ray tubes (CRTs). That's because the costs of recycling these items are more than the value of the component materials that can be extracted from them. This is due in large part to the lack of markets for the recycled glass and plastics in these units. Creating a long term, sustainable recycling infrastructure for the recycling of electronics will require that the electronics are both economically and technologically feasible to recycle. As a result, ISRI decided to support a financial mechanism to cover the negative value of the material.

Manufacturers Should Pay the Costs of Recycling

In looking at the issue, our Electronics Council determined that the best financial mechanism would be for manufacturers to take some responsibility for the cost of recycling their products, by internalizing the cost of collecting, sorting, transporting, and recycling of a defined set of electronics for two primary reasons. First, we recognized that producer responsibility provides a greater incentive to encourage manufacturers to adopt Design For Recycling, a concept that ISRI has been advocating since the early 1980s. Second, we believe that internalization will be cheaper for the consumer/taxpayer. We did not come to this conclusion lightly. In fact, it was a gut-wrenching decision as our industry has long argued that the markets should be allowed to operate freely.

Essentially, Design for Recycling calls upon manufacturers to design their products to be easily recycled at the end of their useful lives, without using hazardous or toxic constituents that can hinder the recycling of those products, and to be manufactured using recycled materials. Design for Recycling contemplates cooperative efforts between manufacturers, recyclers, and the government, in research and development efforts, in defining and understanding the challenges faced at every stage of a product's life cycle, and in mutual efforts to develop better ideas. To date, voluntary calls by the recycling industry to motivate manufacturers to adopt a Design for Recycling philosophy have met with only a tepid response. We do recognize that electronics manufacturers have taken some steps toward designing for recycling; however, there is room for improvement. It is important to understand that greater Design for Recycling can increase recycling productivity that will only ensure a stronger, more sustainable infrastructure.

We believe, as successful businessmen, that if given the flexibility and opportunity to internalize the costs, manufactures can create a model that will be less bureaucratic and burdensome and cheaper for the taxpayer. However, certain manufacturers insist that a consumer tax in the form of an advance recycling fee (ARF), implemented, governed, and administered by state governments, will be cheaper than manufacturers internalizing the costs. We disagree with this logic.

We are aware that there is a fierce and sometimes spirited debate occurring among and between manufacturers and retailers about this issue. This is as it should be. Ultimately, being neither an electronics manufacturer nor a retailer, ISRI's Electronics Council felt it necessary to take an objective look at this issue, as the outcome of the debate will ultimately affect the electronics recyclers.

We acknowledge that some manufacturers have had an unkind, if not visceral, reaction to our position on this issue. They have even questioned our right to have an opinion on the matter of cost internalization versus ARFs. However, while we would not fall on our sword whichever way the Congress or state legislatures decide the cost internalization versus ARF matter, we have specific reasons for holding our preference.

Subsidies Should Not Sustain the Market

While ISRI will ultimately defer to the wisdom of the Congress or the states to decide which financial mechanism is most apt to spur electronic markets, we strongly encourage the Congress and the states to end any financial mechanism as soon as markets for recyclable electronics become economically viable. We are not an industry that looks lightly on government subsidy, and we believe markets must ultimately stand on their own based on solid business principles. That said, whatever financial mechanism the Congress and the states might decide to put forward in order to sustain this market, ISRI suggests that a portion should be applied to the research and development of end-use markets for the materials recovered from electronics products.

Two of the greatest challenges of electronics recycling are the difficulties of sorting the different resins of plastic and recycling chemically coated glass. Targeting funds to further technology in these two fields would have a tremendous impact on making end-use consumer markets more economically viable, which would, over time, ensure these markets could stand on their own without subsidy. In fact, we believe it would be wholly appropriate for the Congress to support research efforts aimed toward the development of technologies for utilizing these materials in the manufacturing process.

What we do not want is an overregulated system that makes it impossible to do our job.

Mr. Chairman, I briefly alluded to RIOS early in my remarks. RIOS is an integrated environmental, health and safety, and quality management system standard that ISRI has developed over. . .18 months. Few industries worldwide have endeavored to undertake such a huge step, but the recycling industry in the United States has always been, and intends to remain, the global leader in recycling technology, environmental protection, worker safety, and the production of high-quality materials. RIOS is a tool for us to accomplish those goals and will help assure that ISRI members who recycle scrap electronics will do so in a manner that is best for our country and the world in which we live.

In closing, I want to remind the committee what this is all about, and that is recycling. At the end of the day when you have done your jobs and the money issue is sorted out, and folks start pulling electronics from closets and basements, it will be the electronics recyclers that end up with electronics on their doorsteps, and that is exactly what we want. What we do not want is an overregulated system that makes it impossible to do our job. Our job is to make sure electronics are properly recycled in order to protect America's environment and support our global economy, I want to thank you Mr. Chairman and members of the committee for addressing this timely issue and welcome any questions you may have.

12

Consumers Should Take Responsibility for Disposing of Cell Phones

Liz Pulliam Weston

Based in Los Angeles, Liz Pulliam Weston writes a nationally syndicated question-and-answer column called "Money Talks." She also writes about personal finance issues for the MSN Money Web site.

With many consumers replacing their cell phones for newer models as often as every eighteen months, the number of discarded phones piling up in the United States is in the hundreds of millions. Rather than throwing old phones away, consumers should find someone willing to buy them, or charitable organizations that can use out-of-fashion phones. Before selling or donating cell phones, however, customers should learn how to perform a "hard reset" to erase data.

Like many of us, Bill Messett had a cell phone graveyard.

His old phones weren't actually dead, but he certainly wasn't using them. Each was tossed into a drawer, along with all its chargers and accessories, when he upgraded to the next model every year or two.

Messett, 38, had the vague idea that he would use the most recent discarded model as a backup in case he lost his current phone. The rest, he sensed, had some value, which made him reluctant to part with them.

Liz Pulliam Weston, "3 Ways to Toss an Old Cell Phone," *MSN Money*, September 11, 2006. http://moneycentral.msn.com. Reproduced by permission of the author.

"I'm kind of packratty in that sense," said Messett, a Miami insurance broker. "I don't like to throw anything away."

Messett found his solution this summer while surfing the Internet. He exchanged two of his newer model phones at RipMobile.com for about $50 in Circuit City gift certificates and donated the rest to RipMobile's affiliated site, Collective-Good in return for a small tax deduction.

New Phones Every Eighteen Months

What to do with old phones is no small issue. The United States alone has more than 200 million cell phone subscribers, and about 5 million of those change carriers each month, which usually means getting a new phone. Even when they don't change carriers, people often change phones to take advantage of improved technology, innovative features and changing fashions.

You should assume that anything with a circuit board, like a phone or a computer, is a caldron of caustic stuff and try to keep it out of the landfill.

"The average user gets a new phone about every 18 months," said James Mosieur, CEO of CellForCash.com. "and they end up retiring the old one."

That's left the United States with hundreds of millions of used cell phones, only a fraction of which have been resold, recycled or reused. Californians, for example, throw away 44,000 cell phones every day.

"Eighty percent have not been repurposed," said Seth Heine, founder and CEO of CollectiveGood/RipMobile, who estimates there are 750 million used cell phones floating around the United States. "They literally go into people's drawers."

Such cell cemeteries are a problem for a number of reasons:

Environmental Concerns

Eventually, owners may get fed up with the clutter and toss their wireless handsets into the nearest trash can—the worst possible outcome.

Cell phones and chargers contain a variety of toxic materials that can poison the soil, water and air. Cell phone manufacturers are trying to make new handsets more environmentally friendly, said Joe Farren, public affairs director for CTIA—The Wireless Association, by phasing out the use of lead and cadmium. Still, you should assume that anything with a circuit board, like a phone or a computer, is a caldron of caustic stuff and try to keep it out of the landfill.

Security Concerns

Today's phones can store all kinds of private data, from passwords to e-mails to that racy photo you snapped of your girlfriend. Anyone who gets his or her hands on your old phone could potentially access this stuff.

Security is an issue for those who would sell or donate phones, too. Trust Digital, which provides mobile security software, recently said it gleaned data from nine of 10 smart phones and personal digital assistants the company purchased on eBay as an experiment. Among the 27,000 pages of data the company retrieved were e-mails between a married man and his girlfriend, details about pending corporate deals and bank account numbers and passwords, according to The Associated Press.

The kind of simple reset users often perform to erase data doesn't scrub the information from many devices' flash memory, the company said. The information can be reclaimed using software available on the Internet. A user needs to perform "an advanced hard reset," which is typically outlined in the phone's user manual, to permanently clear the memory.

Eroding Value

The older the phone, the less it's typically worth. That means fewer shekels in your pocket if you eventually resell and less value to a charity if you decide to donate. If you want the biggest bang for your buck, you should part with an old phone as soon as you get the new one.

CellforCash.com pays anywhere from $5 to $160 for select models, Mosieur said, with the average seller receiving a check for $27. RipMobile.com typically offers more for similar models, with sellers receiving points good toward gift certificates at CircuitCity.com, Starbucks, MSN Music and Karmaloop clothing, among other vendors. CellforCash.com offered $67 for a Treo 650, for example, while RipMobile.com offered $115. On eBay—where about 130,000 used phones change hands each month—a similar model went for just under $200.

Even if a handset has little cash value, it still can benefit charities.

Another option: Check with your carrier. Wireless providers may offer a discount on a new phone—typically $25 or so—when you trade in an older model.

Even if a handset has little cash value, it still can benefit charities. Several posters on the Your Money message board [on the MSN Money Web site] said they donated old phones to battered women's shelters or other nonprofits. "I donate mine to a domestic violence program," wrote poster jlf. "The phones can be used for not only 911, but the women are also given minutes on the phones so that they can be used as a way to contact or be contacted by assistance agencies."

All four major wireless carriers have recycling programs, as do most sites that buy phones, and you can find other drop-off locations through WirelessRecycling.com. These options typically don't provide receipts for tax deductions, however. If that's important, look for sites like CollectiveGood, which recycles phones for charities and which offers tax documentation.

Before you pass on any cell phone, do the following:

- *Discontinue your service.* If you stayed with the same company or ported your phone number to a new provider, service to the old phone has almost certainly been disconnected. Otherwise, you should call your old provider and make sure service is turned off.

- *Do a hard reset on your phone.* This may be more complicated than the simple reset often used to erase data when you're having technical problems with the phone. For example, many Treo phones can be reset by pressing a small button on the back, but a hard reset requires pushing four buttons at once. Check your phone's user manual for the procedure. WirelessRecycling.com also offers instructions on its site for common models.

- *Talk to your company.* Some phones, such as the newest ones running Microsoft's mobile software, can be remotely wiped if the phone is lost or stolen. Other third-party software can delete a phone's information if a specially coded e-mail is delivered to it. Talk to your company about what technology it employs to protect its information and what is available.

13

Consumers Should Consider the Environment When Buying Electronics

Mother Earth News

The environmental magazine Mother Earth News *calls itself "The Original Guide to Living Wisely." Published six times a year, the magazine covers such topics as organic gardening, alternative energy, natural health, and whole foods.*

To keep obsolete computers out of landfills, consumers should buy new machines less frequently, and buy the greenest machines available when it is time to replace them. Proper maintenance will extend the life of a computer, and upgrading an existing computer can in many cases be more practical than buying a new one. When computers must be replaced, consumers should donate their old machines to people who can use them, or look for companies that will recycle them responsibly.

These days, desktop computers seem to be everywhere. They give us access to all kinds of information on a worldwide basis and help us organize our lives as never before. But this convenience comes at a price: Computers are a serious solid waste problem.

Experts estimate that consumers replaced or retired more than 300 million computers over the past decade, and the recycling industry estimates that about 1 billion computers will become potential scrap by 2010. But you can't just toss them in a landfill—they're loaded with toxic chemicals that can potentially leach into groundwater supplies. For example, cathode-ray tube (CRT), or non flat screen, computer monitors can contain 4 to 8 pounds of lead. Relays, switches and liquid crystal display monitors may contain mercury, and plastics used in many computers contain flame retardants that are toxic and persist in the environment—studies suggest they accumulate in the food chain.

Preventive Maintenance to Get the Most Value

By properly caring for your machine, you may be able to extend its life and avoid another toxic contribution to your municipal waste system.

If you need a new computer, consider spending the extra money on an upgradeable machine.

Computers do best in a cool (below 90 degrees), dust-free environment. Dust sucked into the fan can eventually clog the computer and cause overheating, which may burn out a component or cause it to behave erratically.

For obvious reasons, keep food and drinks away. And don't forget to use a surge protector: It not only protects your equipment, but if you turn it off after shutting your computer down, it eliminates the wasted energy of phantom loads (the standby power that your computer draws even when it's off).

Regularly check the space availability on your hard drive to make sure new software or graphics files haven't eaten up your surplus. PC users can do this by choosing "My Computer" from the start menu and right clicking on "Local Disk (C:)," your hard drive. Then select "Properties." Macintosh users can click on the apple icon at the top left corner of their screen and choose "Apple System Profiler." It's also important to keep your virus protection and anti-spyware programs updated.

The best source of help and information is your computer's user manual. If you've misplaced yours, they are easily found online. Simply search for your computer's make and model with the words "owner's manual" or "user's manual.". . .

Buy New, Upgrade, or Buy Used?

Many of us have become resigned to plunking down $600 to $2,000 every two or three years to have a computer that keeps up with the latest games, programs and Web features. If you need a new computer, consider spending the extra money on an upgradeable machine. Computers that cannot be upgraded aren't always cheaper in the long run. They have slower processors and smaller hard drives than other models, as well as less sophisticated keyboards and audio/video components. You also may find it difficult to add features. . . .

Another responsible and affordable choice is to buy a used computer.

An easy way to upgrade is to add a second hard drive or CD burner. New, large applications (100 to 200 MB), a multi-CD game (1 to 2 GB), a collection of MP3 music (500 MB and up), or a couple of hours of digital video (20 to 40 GB) may take more memory than you have. Your desktop PC likely has a space inside called a "drive bay" reserved for a second hard drive, complete with the necessary power and data connectors. You can buy 40- to 300-GB hard drives for less than $1 per GB. If your computer lacks an open bay, consider getting an external hard drive. They cost about $50 more than an internal drive. Be sure to delete all unused programs and files first, though; you might have more room than you thought. . . .

Another responsible and affordable choice is to buy a used computer. Many businesses replace hardware frequently, and there is a growing secondary market for refurbished machines (which sell for as little as $200). Most equipment made after 1999 will meet basic needs—word processing, digital photography, calendars, basic games, etc. . . . Before you buy, try to get a test drive, or check the details on the warranty if you're purchasing from a company. Look for PCs that come with Windows 98 or later, a 500 MHz (or more) processor, 8 GB hard drive, a CD-ROM drive and USB ports. For Macintosh models, be sure they have Mac OS 9 or later.

Promoting Recycling and Greener Computers

In the absence of a federally mandated program, computer recycling is currently a patchwork of initiatives by manufacturers, retailers, and state and local governments. Here's a look at some of the major developments:

Mandatory take-back programs. Laws passed in Maine and California require retailers and manufacturers to take back old computer equipment for recycling. Maine's law requires manufacturers to establish central facilities to collect equipment and to pay for its recycling, which creates an incentive for manufacturers to design equipment that is easy to recycle.

Verified recycling. Recyclers that participate in the Electronics Recycler's Pledge of True Stewardship agree to prevent the use of prison labor, the disposal of waste equipment in ill-equipped municipal facilities, and the export of hazardous computer components to developing countries that lack safe recycling methods. . . .

Taking out toxins. Computer makers are developing new product designs that reduce the use of lead and potentially toxic brominated flame retardants, partly in response to initiatives by the European Union. California [in 2003] passed a ban on the use of some brominated flame retardants after the chemicals were found in fish from the San Francisco Bay.

Creating demand for greener computer desktops, laptops and monitors. Acknowledging the federal government as the largest purchaser of information technology products worldwide, the White House and EPA [in 2004] launched the Federal Electronics Challenge. This voluntary program helps Federal agencies "green" their procurement, use and disposal of electronics. . . .

Defining the word "green." A group of key stakeholders, including government, private, nonprofit and academic representatives, is developing an Electronic Products Environmental Assessment Tool (EPEAT). The goal is to establish a national standard for product assessment and a system to help consumers identify EPEAT-qualified products. . . .

Recycling and Disposal

If possible, find a new home for your old computer. A computer stored in your basement or garage doesn't serve anyone and quickly outlives its usefulness. According to experts at Carnegie Mellon University, PCs lose about 40 percent of their value each year. Many local, regional and national nonprofit organizations will take usable PCs for groups or individuals who can't afford to buy new ones. At TechSoup you can find organizations that will take used equipment, those that offer low-cost refurbished products, and other information.

Some companies also provide discounts on new equipment for customers who send old equipment back for recycling.

If your computer is just too old (that is, it can't run at least Windows 95 or Mac System 7.5), it may be destined for the recycle bin. Check with your local waste management agency to find out if your municipality has a recycling program that accepts electronic waste. Many municipalities in states that have banned computer equipment from landfills offer collection or drop-off programs. Remember to look for a recycling company that has taken the Electronics Recycler's Pledge of True Stewardship.

The company you buy your next computer from may take the old one off your hands, either for free or at a nominal cost. Some companies also provide discounts on new equipment for customers who send old equipment back for recycling. Major manufacturers. with recycling services include Apple, Dell and HP. Some manufacturers also have teamed with retailers such as Best Buy and Office Depot to sponsor in-store collection events. In many cases these services are free, but some retailers may charge fees or accept only certain types or brands of equipment. [In January 2007] Dell launched a carbon offset program called "Plant a Tree for Me" in partnership with two nonprofits, The Conservation Fund and CarbonFund.org. When purchasing a new desktop computer, customers can have a tree planted for a donation of $6, which will compensate for the carbon emissions created by three years' worth of the electricity used by their unit.

Also consider keeping your monitor. Monitors often can be reused even when a computer cannot. If you find no takers for yours, you may want to save it as a spare.

Whatever you do, don't simply take your monitor to the curb for trash pickup. In addition, whether you donate or discard your old computer, be sure to erase all information stored on its hard drive to protect your privacy.

Organizations to Contact

The editors have compiled the following list of organizations concerned with the issues debated in this book. The descriptions are derived from materials provided by the organizations. All have publications or information available for interested readers. The list was compiled on the date of publication of the present volume; the information provided here may change. Be aware that many organizations take several weeks or longer to respond to inquiries, so allow as much time as possible.

Basel Action Network
c/o Earth Economics, 122 South Jackson, Suite 320
Seattle, WA   98104
(206) 652-5555 • Fax: (206) 652-5750
Web site: www.ban.org

The Basal Action Network (BAN) is focused on confronting the global environmental injustice and economic inefficiency of toxic trade (i.e., toxic wastes, products, and technologies) and its devastating impacts. The group actively promotes sustainable and just solutions to the consumption and waste crises, banning waste trade while promoting green, toxic-free, and democratic design of consumer products. BAN's Web site gathers up-to-date e-waste news articles from a variety of international sources and offers a photo gallery, reports, and speeches.

Competitive Enterprise Institute
1001 Connecticut Avenue NW, Suite 1250
Washington, DC   20036
(202) 331-1010 • Fax: (202) 331-0640
E-mail: info@cei.org
Web site: www.cei.org

The Competitive Enterprise Institute (CEI), founded in 1984, is a nonprofit public-policy organization dedicated to advancing the principles of free enterprise and limited government.

CEI argues that the best solutions to environmental problems come from individuals making their own choices in a free marketplace. It publishes opinion and analysis pieces on its online "Daily Update" and the electronic newsletter *CEI Planet.*

Ecology Action

P.O. Box 1188, Santa Cruz, CA   95061-1188
(831) 426-5925 • Fax: (831) 425-1404
Web site: www.ecoact.org

Established in 1970, Ecology Action is a nonprofit environmental consultancy delivering education services, technical assistance, and program implementation for initiatives that assist individuals, business, and government in the Santa Cruz, California, area to maximize environmental quality and community well-being. Although many of its programs are locally based, Ecology Action's "e-Waste Electronic Recycling Program" Web page offers educational information, press releases, and links to national electronics manufacturers' recycling programs.

Greenpeace

702 H Street NW, Washington, DC   20001
(202) 462-1177
E-mail: info@wdc.greenpeace.org
Web site: www.greenpeace.org/usa/campaigns/toxics

Founded in 1971, Greenpeace is an international organization that uses peaceful direct action and creative communication to address global environmental problems. Greenpeace releases an annual "Guide to Greener Electronics," which ranks consumer electronics companies based on the removal of toxic chemicals from their products and company recycling initiatives.

Grist

710 Second Avenue, Suite 860, Seattle, WA   98104
(206) 876-2020 • Fax: (253) 423-6487

E-mail: grist@grist.org
Web site: www.grist.org

Grist is a nonprofit environmental news, commentary, and humor organization funded by foundation grants, reader contributions, and advertising. Its slogan is "Grist: it's gloom and doom with a sense of humor. So laugh now—or the planet gets it." Grist's Web site features editorials and news articles about environmental topics including e-waste and recycling, podcasts, an advice column, and a blog.

Institute of Scrap Recycling Industries
1615 L Street NW, Suite 600, Washington, DC 20036-5610
(202) 662-8500 • Fax: (202) 626-0900
Web site: www.isri.org

The Institute of Scrap Recycling Industries (ISRI) is the voice of the scrap recycling industry, representing more than 1,350 private, for-profit companies that process, broker, and industrially consume scrap commodities. The group works to encourage manufacturers to build electronics with safer, more easily recyclable materials and educates the public about the benefits of scrap recycling. ISRI publishes a bimonthly magazine, *Scrap*, and maintains a collection of reports, letters, and position papers on its Web site.

National Recycling Coalition
1325 G Street NW, Suite 1025, Washington, DC 20005
(202) 347-0450 • Fax: (202) 347-0449
E-mail: info@nrc-recycle.org
Web site: www.nrc-recycle.org

The National Recycling Coalition (NRC) is a nonprofit organization dedicated to the advancement and improvement of recycling, source reduction, composting, and reuse. Founded in 1978, NRC's objective is to eliminate waste and promote sustainable economies through advancing sound management practices for raw materials in North America. It provides technical information, education, and advocacy services to recycling companies. NRC's Web site provides tips for spokespeople, including "20 Press Release Ideas to Promote Recycling," and the organization gathers news stories about recycling.

Swiss Federal Institute of Technology
ETH Zurich, HG, Rämistrasse 101, Zurich   8092
   Switzerland
+41-4463211-11 • Fax: +41-4463210-10
Web site: http://ewasteguide.info

Through a program called Empa, the Swiss Federal Institute of Technology is a pioneer in monitoring and controlling e-waste management systems. Empa leads several projects in Asia, Africa, and Latin America, helping to build capacities for e-waste management in areas of policy and legislation, business and finance, and technology and skills. It has been instrumental in helping to develop a global knowledge-sharing platform on e-waste. It maintains an extensive "e-waste guide" on the Web, offering statistics, reports, bibliography, and link to subscribe to an e-mail newsletter.

U.S. Environmental Protection Agency (EPA)
Office of Solid Waste (5305P)
1200 Pennsylvania Avenue NW, Washington, DC   20460
Web site: www.epa.gov/ecycling

Established in 1970, the U.S. Environmental Protection Agency (EPA) leads the nation's environmental science, research, education, and assessment efforts. The EPA maintains a page dedicated to "ecycling" on its Web site, offering basic information about reducing electronic waste, frequent questions and answers about electronic waste, publications that provide information about electronic waste, related links that include resources for recycling and donation programs, and information about market trends in electronic waste generation and recovery.

Zero Waste America
Lynn Landes, 217 South Jessup Street
Philadelphia, PA   19107
(215) 629-3553
E-mail: lynnlandes@earthlink.net
Web site: http://zerowasteamerica.org/zwa/index.html

Zero Waste America (ZWA) is a Internet-based environmental research organization that provides information on legislative, legal, technical, environmental, health, and consumer issues. ZWA specializes in information on U.S. waste disposal issues, particularly the lack a federal waste management plan, the use of disposal bans to stop waste disposal and imports, the proposed federal interstate waste legislation, waste data collection methodology, and applicable federal case law. Its Web site offers photos, analysis of successful and unsuccessful recycling plans, and links to sources of news about waste.

Bibliography

Books

Mary Ann Bell, Bobby Ezell, and James L. Van Roeckel — *Cybersins and Digital Good Deeds: A Book About Technology and Ethics.* New York: Haworth, 2007.

Kevin Brigden, Iryana Labunska, David Santillo, and M. Allsopp — *Recycling of Electronic Wastes in China and India: Workplace and Environmental Contamination.* Exeter, UK: Greenpeace International, 2005.

Sheila Davis and Ted Smith — *Corporate Strategies for Electronics Recycling: A Tale of Two Systems.* San Jose, CA: Silicon Valley Toxics Coalition, 2003.

Bette K. Fishbein — *Waste in the Wireless World: The Challenge of Cell Phones.* New York: Inform, 2002.

Elizabeth Grossman — *High Tech Trash: Digital Devices, Hidden Toxics, and Human Health.* Washington, DC: Island Press, 2006.

Greg Kennedy — *An Ontology of Trash: The Disposable and Its Problematic Nature.* Albany: State University of New York Press, 2008.

Michael S. Malone — *The Valley of Heart's Delight: A Silicon Valley Notebook 1963–2001.* New York: Wiley, 2002.

James E.
McCarthy

Recycling Computers and Electronic Equipment: Legislative and Regulatory Approaches for "E-Waste." Washington, DC: Congressional Information Service, Library of Congress, 2005.

David Naguib and Lisa Sun-Hee Park

The Silicon Valley of Dreams: Environmental Injustice, Immigrant Workers, and the High-Tech Global Economy. New York: New York University Press, 2002.

Heather Rogers

Gone Tomorrow: The Hidden Life of Garbage. New York: Norton, 2005.

Elizabeth Royte

Garbage Land: On the Secret Trail of Trash. New York: Little, Brown, 2005.

Nicky Scott

Reduce, Reuse, Recycle: An Easy Household Guide. White River Junction, VT: Chelsea Green Publishing, 2007.

Giles Slade

Technology and Obsolescence in America. Cambridge, MA: Harvard University Press, 2006.

Periodicals

Zeina Al Hajj

"It's 'Cool' to Be Digital—But Don't Overlook the Costs." *Financial Times* (London), February 11, 2008.

Dominic Ali

"Future Shock: Is Newer Technology Worth the Trash?" *Owl*, May 2007.

Gabriella Boston   "Saving Earth One Circuit Board and TV at a Time." *Washington Times*, January 31, 2008.

Terence Chea   "Recycling of E-Waste Becomes Global Problem." *Newsday*. November 25, 2007.

Timothy Chui   "Vista Opens Up Windows into E-Waste Nightmare." *The Standard* (London), January 29, 2007.

Dan Costa   "Plant a Tree for Me." *PC Magazine*, March 20, 2007.

Steve Dow   "Left on the Scrap Heap." *Sydney Morning Herald*, May 29, 2007.

Dana Joel Gattuso   "Costly Hysteria on 'E-Waste.'" *EnviroWire*, March 14, 2005.

Elizabeth Grossman   "Where Computers Go to Die— and Kill." *Salon.com*, April 10, 2006. www.salon.com.

Jess Hemerly   "Apple Computers: Fun for You, Toxic for the Environment." *AlterNet*, January 30, 2007. www.alternet.org.

Robert Houghton   "Realizing Our Best Intentions." *Recycling Today*, July 2006.

Jennifer Hughes   "A Central Stop for All That Hazardous Waste." *New York Times*, May 6, 2007.

Anne Kandra   "A Computer Is a Terrible Thing to Waste." *PC World*, January 2005.

Andrew Leonard   "The Circuit Board Bakers of Guiyu." *Salon.com*, November 7, 2007. www.salon.com.

Adam Minter   "China's Huge Hunger for Scrap." *Wall Street Journal*, March 25, 2004.

Jon Mooallem   "The Afterlife of Cellphones." *New York Times*, January 13, 2008.

Elizabeth Armstrong Moore   "Momentum Builds for 'Revolution' to Recycle Electronic Waste." *Christian Science Monitor*, July 31, 2006.

Susan Moran   "Panning E-Waste for Gold." *New York Times*, May 17, 2006.

Mary K. Pratt   "Pan-Africa: Computer Donations Finding Their Way to Toxic Waste Dumps." *Africa News*, March 9, 2006.

"Tech Trash: Still Stinking Up the Corporate Landscape." *Computerworld*, March 26, 2007.

Elizabeth Royte   "E-Waste @ Large." *New York Times*, January 27, 2006.

Giles Slade   "Ten Thousand Songs in Your Pocket. Ten Thousand Years in a Landfill." *Mother Jones*, March/April 2007.

Michelle Slatalla   "On Gadget Overload and Feeling Powerless." *New York Times*, January 3, 2008.

Jennifer Smith   "Not as Simple as the Recycle Bin."
                        Newsday (New York), January 14,
                        2008.

Beverly Thorpe   "Unplugged: Canada Should Follow
                        Europe's Lead on E-Waste." *Alterna-
                        tives Journal*, January 2006.

Moises   "How Do You Make Electronics
Velasquez-Manoff   Easier to Recycle?" *Christian Science
                        Monitor*, March 8, 2007.

Rob Walker   "Many Unhappy Returns." *New York
                        Times*, January 6, 2008.

Maura Welch   "Where Computers Go to Die." *Bos-
                        ton Globe*, April 17, 2006.

Nigel Whitfield   "Our PCs, Our Planet." *Personal
                        Computer World*, August 17, 2006.

Lorraine Woellert   "HP Wants Your Old PCs Back."
                        Business Week, April 10, 2006.

Index